minnies

quickknits for babies and toddlers

A MINNOWKNITS BOOK

Jil Eaton

Contemporary Books

Chicago New York San Francisco Lisbon London Madrid Mexico City
Milan New Delhi San Juan Seoul Singapore Sydney Toronto

Library of Congress Cataloging-in-Publication Data

Eaton, Jill, 1949–
    Minnies : QuickKnits for babies and toddlers / Jill Eaton.
        p.   cm.
    Includes index.
    ISBN 0-8092-9698-5
    1. Knitting—Patterns.   2. Children's clothing.   I. Title.

TT825 .E2798   2001
746.43′20432—dc21   2001019212

Contemporary Books

A Division of The McGraw-Hill Companies

1 2 3 4 5 6 7 8 9 0 SSI/SSI 0 9 8 7 6 5 4 3 2 1

ISBN 0-8092-9698-5

This book was set in Scala Sans
Printed and bound by Star Standard Industries

Cover and interior design by Kim Bartko
Interior photographs by Nina Van Brocklin Fuller
Learn-to-knit illustrations by Joni Coniglio
Schematics by Elizabeth Berry

McGraw-Hill books are available at special quantity discounts to use as premiums and
sales promotions, or for use in corporate training programs. For more information, please
write to the Director of Special Sales, Professional Publishing, McGraw-Hill, Two Penn
Plaza, New York, NY 10121-2298. Or contact your local bookstore.

To my son,

Alexander Lord Eaton,

my original inspiration

contents

preface   vi

hello, baby   vii

tricks of the trade   viii

knitting ABCs—a refresher   xxiv

pip-squeaks
    layette with panache!   1
        koko kimono   2
        puff baby   8
        baby bunting   12
        feltie feet   18
        welcome, baby   22

jeepers creepers
    play clothes with dash and flair   29
        swing set   30
        seedling   36
        flax jax   40
        cable-alls   46
        dutch treat   52

brrrr . . .

warm wonders for crispy days 59

    genghis baby 60

    jump 64

    baby baby 70

    snow baby 76

    piccolo 80

zing! 85

zany, colorful delights

    vestimenti 86

    gelati 90

    feltie chapeau 94

    english trifle 98

    mini pini 102

    colori 106

merci mille fois 111

shopping notes 118

books of note 122

short stuff 124

needle conversions 125

index 127

preface

Ah, babies. Pip-squeaks and puddle-jumpers, peepers and creepers. . . . Minnies! What joy, what love, what fun to have and hold, to cuddle and snuggle. Everyone loves babies. And we love to knit for them, for instant gratification all around. Expectant mothers, grandmothers, aunties, and friends, all whipping up quick confections in fluffy angora, velvety cashmere, soft cotton, and warm wools the minute the news is out.

Icy pinks and tender greens sashay with unexpected brights, adorable tender combinations for cherished heirlooms. So lullaby those babies, and knit to your heart's delight!

Remember, when we are knitting, all is right with the world.

Jil Eaton

hello, baby

When I had my son, Alexander, fifteen years ago, I returned to knitting with great enthusiasm. I soon found, however, that most patterns called for fingering weight yarns and size 2 needles, making it practically impossible to finish the sweaters before he was born. So I began working up my own designs, and Minnow-Knits was born right along with Alexander!

Minnies is a collection of delectable fashions for babies—twenty-one chic projects and charming QuickKnits sized for newborn, 1, 2, and 3 years. Sweaters and dresses and rompers and booties, buntings and jackets and overalls and caps, everything your own special baby needs for cozy comfort. Using sport weight to chunky yarns in the best fibers and blends allows even new mothers to find the time to knit more than one of these tiny darling garments.

When I'm designing any pattern, I always have it knit in the smallest size as a proto-type, checking details, shaping, and the overall look of the piece. These tiny newborn garments are so fetching they have become the inspiration for this new collection. Combining my trademark simple silhouettes with the best in fibers, clear rich colors, and offbeat details makes this a collection of baby clothes with panache, easily and quickly knit.

Organized by category, Minnies includes layette, play clothes, cold-weather wear, and witty confections! Knitting tips and technical information are included, as well as "Knitting ABCs—a Refresher."

Each garment was photographed flat in the studio to allow knitters a clear view of all the shaping and details. Photographs of the babies and toddlers were shot sometimes on location and sometimes in the studio, showing you the garments on these little cherubs in live action and living color. As always, yardage is given both in English and metric, to allow you flexibility and to encourage individual creativity.

tricks of the trade

One of the best reasons in the world to begin knitting is the arrival of a new baby. Knitting small-size baby garments gives us instant pleasure, as we whip up one sweater or hat after another. The smallest gauge I use is sport weight, and many of these garments are worsted or even bulky weight; the Baby Bunting is done on doubled bulky yarn, and you can easily knit it in a weekend. Knitting baby items gives you great flexibility, as the small size is so easily portable, perfect for the car or plane, waiting room or meeting.

I believe knitting is magic, a Zen-like way to calm down and meditate, a simple way to find clear just-for-yourself time. Knitting allows us to be productive while relaxing at the same time! Here are a few of my trade secrets and technical tips for you as you knit, knit, knit!

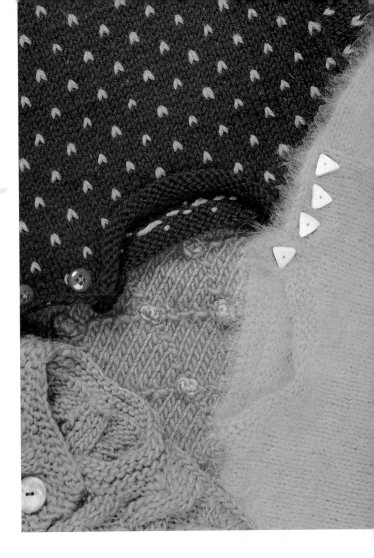

I *always* use the most beautiful yarns I can find, and I believe you should always honor your handwork with the best in materials. I love wool for its warmth, elasticity, durability, and ability to hold beautiful dyes. Cottons now are really great, holding their shape and color. Cotton breathes and is comfortable in a great range of weather and climates. It is cool and durable, usually washable, and perfect for long-wearing garments. The new blends and synthetic chenilles are fabulous, especially for babies. I even have included a brand-new nylon chenille, soft as clouds and quick to knit. Quite a delight!

My patterns are always generic, with the required amounts for every garment given in yards and meters. You can substitute yarn colors and weights by doing just a bit of math, and your yarn shops can easily help you. (But make sure you do your swatch, and get your gauge!) I also give the yarns that I have used for each knitted sample, so you can find the exact colors and weights; you also might want to experiment, choosing your own creative palette. But *always* use the very best yarns you can afford, in natural fibers and blends. Yarns today are wonderful, washable, and durable—just the thing for heirlooms.

KNITTING SUPPLIES

The following essentials will really make a difference in your knitting life!

Knitting Kit

I recommend a clear, zippered plastic case as the perfect knitting kit, holding the following items:

- Small, sharp scissors
- Yarn needles (I like Chibi needles with bent tips best)

- Measuring tape (I like the retractable kind)
- Yarn T-pins and safety pins for marking or holding dropped stitches
- Stitch holders, both short and long
- Stitch markers (split-rings are my favorites as they can be easily moved)
- Cable needles (my favorites are straight)
- Small calculator (Invaluable!)
- Point protectors, both large and small, to keep your work on the needles

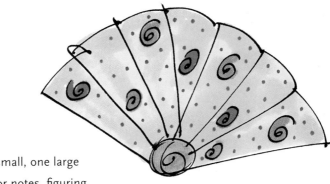

Row counter

Needle/gauge ruler

Crochet hooks, one small, one large

Pen and notebook, for notes, figuring,
and design

Knitting Bag or Basket

I have many—usually one in each room of
my house, two for traveling, and larger ones
for the studio. I love lightweight mesh bags
for traveling, as the yarn can get heavy, and
baskets can be bulky. Use whatever carryall
you like, but dedicate it to your projects and
you'll always have everything at hand.

Needles

You will, sooner or later, want a complete set
of needles, with doubles in your favorite
sizes. I use different needles for various
projects depending on the yarn or garment.

BASIC NEEDLES Swallow casein needles
are wonderful, warm in your hand,
silent, and available in many beautiful
colors, in 9" / 23 cm, 12" / 30 cm, and
14" / 35 cm. Fabulous, and perfect

for basic two-needle knitting. I always favor
the shortest needles possible, which puts
less strain on your wrists.

Swallow needles come in beautiful
tortoise, as well as in vibrant colors in the
12" / 30 cm size.

CIRCULAR NEEDLES Addi Turbo circular
knitting needles are billed as the "amazing
turbos," which is perfectly accurate! Made of
silver-plated brass that is easy in your hands,
soft and quiet, Addi needles actually speed
up your knitting time. The soft cords let
stitches glide quickly along the needles,
without snags or catches to slow you down.
I use Addi circulars often, simply working
back and forth rather than around when
appropriate. Addi Turbo circulars are sized
from 12" to 60", from US size 00 to 36,
easily accommodating any project. So
smooth, so fast to work with, quiet and
flexible, just a joy to have in your hands.

DOUBLE POINTED NEEDLES For these pokey pointed sets, I love both Swallow casein and bamboo. They are as light as air and stay put as you rotate your work. I always carry some in my knitting kit, for easy emergency repair and as temporary stitch holders.

Needle Cases

If you begin using needle cases, your needles will be in one place, organized and accessible when you need them. Cases for both straight and circulars are readily available in knitting shops, in a variety of styles and sizes. Whatever your preference, get some cases and get organized!

Knitting Notebook

All my knitting design students are required to keep a three-ring binder, to organize patterns and projects. Clear three-ring pages that open at the top are perfect, and I always keep the pattern, notes, and a small amount of the remaining yarn. The yarn is perfect for later repairs, and the notebook makes a keepsake diary of your projects. You'll be surprised how fast your projects mount up, and how much fun it is to remember the garments long after they've left your hands.

Yarn Winder

A table-mounted yarn winder is a great luxury. They are found in your favorite

knitting shop or catalog, and save hours
of time winding hanks of yarn. Unless of
course you love that yarn-winding ritual, too!

Knitting Lights

Good light is essential, and I love the kind of
lights you can pull down over your work. I
have a dedicated knitting light in every room
where I knit. A high-intensity, adjustable light
will save you many hours of mistakes on
your handwork, saving you from headaches,
both physical and mental!

MADE TO MEASURE

Always measure the individual you are
knitting for! This may seem simplistic, but I
have found that often the simplest bits get
overlooked. It is very easy to alter a pattern,
making shorter or longer sleeves or bodice,
and specific lengths make knitting easy.
When knitting sleeves from the shoulder
down, as I usually do, make any length
adjustments at the top of the sleeve. If
the lucky individual being knit for is not
available, measure a garment that fits that

person comfortably. I recommend knitting a size up if the measurements fall between sizes, because children grow at an alarming rate. When knitting for an expected baby or new arrival, the newborn to 3 month size will fit right away, but for a very short time. This size is perfect for shower and birth presents, darling tiny garments. The 1-year size is generally a safe place to begin knitting for new arrivals if you want the garment to have some longevity. My template is generous, and many of my patterns are QK, or QuickKnit, quick and simple to knit; even so, you may be surprised by the growth rate of your babies and toddlers.

NOTE The patterns in the heavier weight yarns in this book often include selvage stitches on each side. These stitches are not included in final measurements, as they are taken up in the seam.

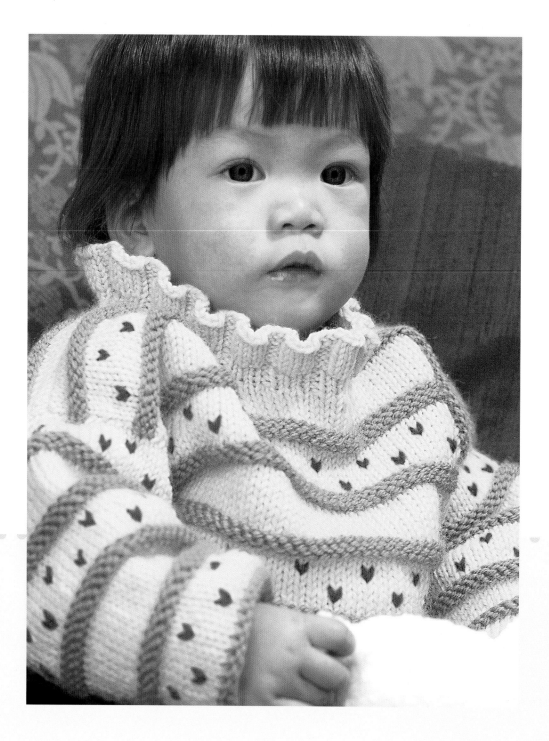

MEASURE UP!

The following will help you measure your child, which along with getting your gauge will be a giant step toward a garment that fits perfectly.

A. For hats, measure the widest part of the head, just above the ears.

B. CBS, or center-back-sleeve. Measure from the middle of the back straight across to the wrist. This figure will tell you how to adjust the sleeve length, no matter what the design.

C. The chest measurement is probably the most important. Measure around the chest about 1" / 2.5 cm down from the arm. You might also want to measure a garment that fits your child comfortably around the chest to aid in finding the correct size.

D. Waist measurement.

E. Shoulder to waist shows the torso length, useful for adjustments in overall garment length.

F. For tunics or longer sweaters, knowing this measurement lets you knit the garment accordingly.

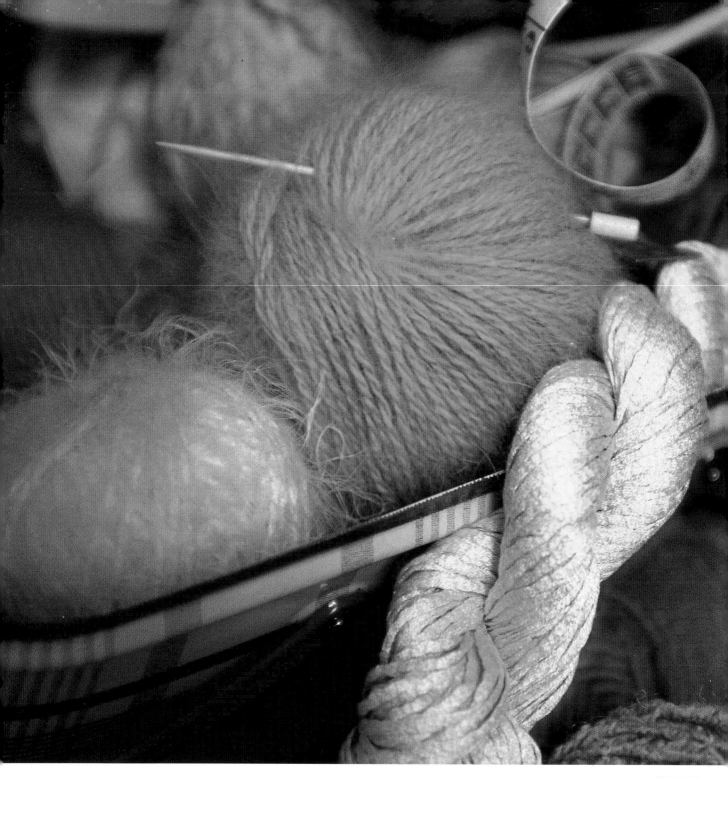

KNITTING TO FIT

My mantra, the backbone of my design classes, and the most important thing you can do if you want your garments to fit properly, is to knit a gauge swatch. If you want your garments to fit, just do your swatch! You might think that if you are knitting for babies gauge doesn't matter, but it does make a big difference. The correct gauge allows you to make a fabric that is even and smooth, with the correct drape and hand, never mind being the correct size.

As you progress with your talents, you will find that knitting the gauge swatch is a very creative part of the project, the point where you make all your design decisions for each particular garment. My colors are a starting point, and you may delight in discovering your own new combinations. You may mix and match yarns, as long as you "get your gauge"!

GAUGE SWATCH

A gauge swatch takes a very short time to knit but gives you all the information you need to knit a piece that will fit the way you want and expect. Your gauge swatch then becomes part of your knitting history, and gives you an extra bit of yarn for emergencies.

I know many of you skip your gauge swatch, especially for newborn projects. But getting the correct gauge will make all the difference in the success of your knitting.

Your gauge, or the correct number of stitches per inch or centimeter, and the correct number of rows called for in the pattern, is crucial to the success of your knitting project. For instance, knitting at even a half-stitch off gauge will make a significant difference in the final measure-ment of your garment. If the pattern calls for 100 stitches, at 5 stitches to the inch, and you are actually getting 5.5 stitches to the inch, your sweater will measure 18 inches instead of 20. Two inches is a big difference, especially on a baby!

Using the needles suggested in the pattern, cast on the correct number of stitches to make a 4″ / 10 cm swatch, plus 6. Knit 3 rows. Always knit 3 stitches at the beginning and end of every row and work

straight in the pattern stitches called for until the piece measures 4″ / 10 cm; then knit 3 rows and bind off. Lay the swatch on a flat, smooth surface. Measure inside the garter stitch frame; you should have 4″ / 10 cm exactly. If your swatch is too big, or you have too few stitches per inch or centimeter, change to a needle one size smaller. If your swatch is too small, or there are too many stitches per inch or centimeter, change to the next larger needles. Changing one size at a time, keep going until you get the correct gauge. The number of stitches per inch or centimeter is the most important; if the row gauge is eluding you, you can adjust as you work through the pattern.

I consistently knit fast and loose, and now always begin my swatch with needles one size smaller than those recommended in the pattern or on the yarn ball band. Remember, these are *recommendations* only, as we all knit differently with various needles and yarns. Always do your gauge with the needles you will be using for the project, too . . . there can be a difference in gauge between plastic, metal, or bamboo needles on the exact same yarn! And check your gauge again after working about 4" / 10 cm, just to be sure you're getting the gauge. Getting into the habit of doing your gauge swatch will fine tune your craftsmanship, making you a better knitter for life.

ROW COUNTING

If you count your rows, you will have a perfectly matching front and back, or two exact sleeves. I always include row counts in my gauge section for every pattern, and you can always count based on the garment chart. If you stretch one piece to match another, the resulting pull will bother you when the garment is finished. My motto is "when in doubt, tear it out" if it's not perfect. So count your rows for perfect results and easy finishing.

FINISHING

In every book I say: *Finish in the morning, in good light, on a flat surface.* Period.

Finishing the knitting is one thing, but finishing the actual garment is another exacting task, requiring rested concentration and attention to detail. We all want to quickly sew up a garment the minute it is off the needles, but good finishing can mean the difference between a beautiful piece and a mediocre effort, so wait until you're fresh and able.

I usually design sweaters with sleeves knit from the shoulder down, using a knitted shoulder seam bind-off. This technique is worked with *wrong sides facing* resulting in a neat seam on the outside of the shoulder ridge. This seam finishing gives the shoulder stability, as well as being a design statement. Then you only have to sew sleeve and side seams, and voilà!

TIP When you are adding colors or the next ball of yarn, always leave a 6" / 15 cm length, which will make the weaving-in at the end much easier.

BLOCKING

When your knitting is complete, weave in all the loose tails of yarn on each piece. Cover

each piece with two damp towels, one under and one over, pinning pieces in place. Or pin to a blocking board, which is available through catalogs and yarn shops. Lightly steam at the appropriate setting, and dry flat on a towel, rack, or a blocking board/table if you have one. Blocking usually improves the look of your garment, as long as it is gently done, without crushing the fibers. Be gentle.

LAUNDERING

Gauge swatches come in very handy for testing washability, following the yarn label instructions. I also find many yarns are machine washable, if you put them on a very gentle cycle in tepid water in a small mesh bag, which holds their shape and gets them really clean. For wool, you can also use a no-rinse sweater soap such as Eucalan, available at fine yarn shops. Fill your washer with tepid (not cold) water, and add the laundry product. Soak the garment for 10 minutes; then go directly to the spin cycle, spin, remove, and block as usual.

If you take care of your hand-knits, they will take care of your babies for many years!

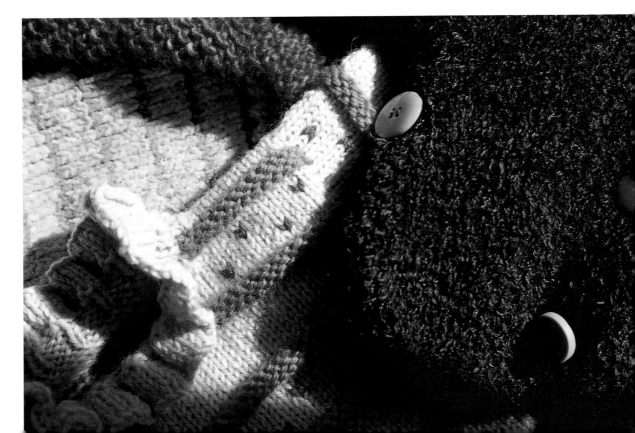

knitting ABCs—a refresher

Many of us return to knitting—or even begin knitting—when a new baby appears in the family. I've always found that knitting gives us a productive way to relax, all the while creating unique fashions. Baby clothes are the best, especially for new or returning knitters, as the time element is greatly reduced. For instance, a baby hat can be whipped up in a few hours, and even the sweaters in this collection are QuickKnits. The Baby Bunting can be knit easily in a weekend, perfect for that last-minute baby shower gift! So often I hear that you would love to knit, but. . . . Just pick up some needles and give it a go. I think you'll be surprised how easy and rewarding it is.

This learn-to-knit refresher section takes you through the basic elements of knitting. I know many of you have been knitters in the past, and now want to begin the craft anew, or are simply just beginner knitters, so here is an illustrated guide to knitting. I have described the easiest type of cast on, the knit-on method. Once you have mastered this method, you have actually learned the basic knit stitch.

SLIP KNOT

1. Hold the yarn in the left hand, leaving a short length free. Wrap the yarn from the skein into a circle and bring the yarn from below and up through the center of the circle. Insert the needle under this strand as shown.

2. Pull on both the short and long ends to tighten the knot on the needle.

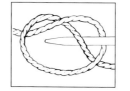 

STEP 1. Slip knot   **STEP 2.** Slip knot

CAST ON

1. Hold the needle with the slip knot in the left hand and the empty needle in the right hand. Insert the right needle from front to back under the left needle and through the stitch. With the yarn in the right hand, wrap the yarn around the right needle as shown.

2. With the tip of the right needle, pull the wrap through the stitch on the left needle and bring to the front.

3. Slip the new stitch off of the left needle and onto the right needle. Repeat steps 1 to 3 for a simple knit-on cast on. (For an alternate, more advanced method, continue on to step 4.)

4. Insert the right needle between the first two stitches on left needle and wrap the yarn around the needle as shown. Repeat steps 2 to 4 for the alternate method, called cable cast on.

BASIC KNIT STITCH

1. Hold the needle with the cast-on stitches in the left hand and hold the empty needle in the right hand. Insert the right needle from front to back into the first stitch on the left needle and wrap the yarn just like in the first step of the cast on.

2. With the tip of the right needle, pull the wrap through the stitch on the left needle and

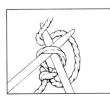

STEP 1. Cast on

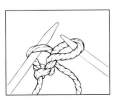

STEP 2. Cast on

STEP 3. Cast on

STEP 4. Cast on

STEP 1. Basic knit stitch

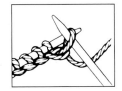

STEP 2. Basic knit stitch

onto the right needle. Drop the stitch from the left needle. A new stitch is made on the right needle. Repeat steps 1 and 2 until all the stitches from the left needle are on the right needle. Turn the work and hold the needle with the new stitches in the left hand and continue knitting back and forth.

BASIC PURL STITCH

The purl stitch is basically the opposite of the knit stitch. Instead of pulling the wrapped yarn toward you, you will push it through the back of the stitch. Because it is harder to see what you are doing, the purl stitch is a bit harder to learn than the knit stitch. When you knit

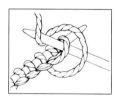

Basic purl stitch

one row, then purl one row, you create the stockinette stitch.

Hold the needle with the cast-on stitches in the left hand, and hold the empty needle in the right hand. Insert the right needle from back to front, into the first stitch on the left needle, and wrap the yarn counterclockwise around the needle as shown. With the tip of the right needle, pull the wrap through the stitch on the left needle and onto the right needle, as in the knit stitch. Drop the stitch from the left needle. A new stitch is made on the right needle. Continue in this way across the row.

STOCKINETTE STITCH

On straight needles, knit on the right side, purl on the wrong side. On a circular needle, knit every row.

GARTER STITCH

When using straight needles, knit every row. On a circular needle, knit one row, purl one row.

KNIT 2 TOGETHER (K2TOG), OR DECREASE

Hold the needle with the knitted fabric in the left hand and hold the empty needle in theright hand. Insert the right needle from front to back through the first two stitches on the left needle. Wrap the yarn and pull through the two stitches as if knitting. Drop the two stitches from the left needle. One new stitch is made from two stitches; therefore one stitch is decreased.

INCREASE

The most common way to increase is to knit in the front of the stitch, and, without removing the stitch from the left-hand needle, knit in the back of the same stitch, then drop the stitches from the left needle. This makes two stitches in one stitch.

BIND OFF

Hold the needle with the knitting in the left hand and hold the empty needle in the right hand. Knit the first two stitches. * With the left needle in front of the right needle, insert the tip of the left needle into the second stitch on the right needle and pull it over the first stitch and off the right needle. One stitch has been bound off. Knit the next stitch, then repeat from the * until all the stitches are bound off.

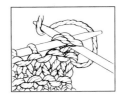

Knit 2 together

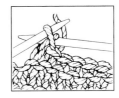

Bind off

pip-squeaks
layette with panache!

The pending birth of a tiny tot is music to a

knitter's ears . . . the needles and yarn come

flying out the second we hear the news. How

can we resist? Angora and chenille and silk

and soft cotton creating blissful confections

for baby. Splurge on one of these tiny delights,

or whip them all up in time for baby's arrival!

koko kimono

double-breasted baby kimono with i-cord ties
in silk-soft rayon • unisex • quickknit

Using silklike rayon yarn, this traditionally styled kimono is simple to knit in stockinette stitch. Perfect for the newborn set, this is a delightful shower gift, too. A kimono dresses up the diaper ensemble, a party sweater for babies with style.

SIZES

To fit newborn to 3 months (6 months - 18 months)
Finished chest (closed): 19 (20 - 22)″ / 48 (50.5 - 56) cm
Length, shoulder to hem: 9½ (10½ - 11½)″ / 24 (26.5 - 29) cm

MATERIALS

DK weight yarn which will obtain gauge given below
300 (370 - 450) yd. / 275 (340 - 410) m
Knitting needles, size 6 US (8 UK, 4 mm) or size needed to obtain gauge
Double pointed needles (dpns), size 6 US (8 UK, 4 mm)
Stitch holders and markers
Sample in photograph knit in Berroco Glace in #2500 Seafoam

GAUGE

22 sts and 28 rows = 4″ / 10 cm over St st using size 6 US (8 UK, 4 mm) needles
Always check gauge to save time and to ensure correct yardage and correct fit!

BACK

Cast on 52 (55 - 61) sts. K 4 rows, then work in St st until piece measures 9½ (10½ - 11½)" / 24 (26.5 - 29) cm from beg, end with a WS row. Work 16 (16 - 19) sts and place on a holder for right shoulder, bind off next 20 (23 - 23) sts for back neck, work rem sts and place on a 2nd holder for left shoulder.

LEFT FRONT

Cast on 41 (42 - 45) sts. K 4 rows. *Next row (RS):* Work in St st to last 2 sts, work last

2 sts in garter st. Cont as established until piece measures 6½ (7½ - 8½)" / 16.5 (19 - 21.5) cm from beg, end with a WS row.
Shape neck: *Dec row 1 (RS):* Work to last 4 sts, k2tog, k2. Work 1 row even. *Dec row 2:* Work to last 5 sts, k3tog, k2. [Work 1 row even. Rep dec row 1] 4 times. *Next row (WS):* Bind off 8 sts, work to end. Cont to bind off from neck edge 5 sts once, 3 sts 1 (2 - 2) times, 2 sts 1 (0 - 0) time. When same length as back, place rem 16 (16 - 19) sts on holder.

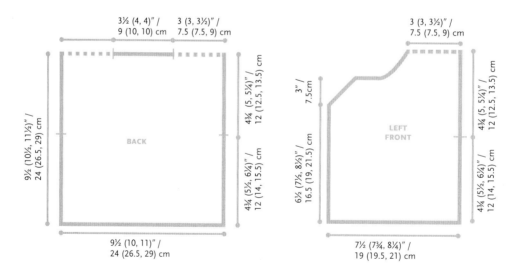

BACK

3½ (4, 4)" / 9 (10, 10) cm   3 (3, 3½)" / 7.5 (7.5, 9) cm

4¾ (5, 5¼)" / 12 (12.5, 13.5) cm

9½ (10½, 11½)" / 24 (26.5, 29) cm

4¾ (5½, 6¼)" / 12 (14, 15.5) cm

9½ (10, 11)" / 24 (26.5, 29) cm

LEFT FRONT

3 (3, 3½)" / 7.5 (7.5, 9) cm

4¾ (5, 5¼)" / 12 (12.5, 13.5) cm

3" / 7.5cm

6½ (7½, 8½)" / 16.5 (19, 21.5) cm

4¾ (5½, 6¼)" / 12 (14, 15.5) cm

7½ (7¾, 8¼)" / 19 (19.5, 21) cm

RIGHT FRONT

Cast on 26 (27 - 30) sts. K 4 rows. *Next row (RS):* Work 2 sts in garter st, work in St st to end. Cont as established until piece measures 8½ (9½ - 10½)" / 21.5 (24 - 26.5) cm from beg, end with a WS row. **Shape neck:** *Next row (RS):* Bind off 5 (6 - 6) sts (neck edge), k to end. Cont to bind off from neck edge 3 sts once, 2 sts once. When same length as back, place rem 16 (16 - 19) sts on holder.

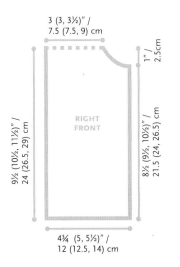

3 (3, 3½)" / 7.5 (7.5, 9) cm

1" / 2.5cm

9½ (10½, 11½)" / 24 (26.5, 29) cm

RIGHT FRONT

8½ (9½, 10½)" / 21.5 (24, 26.5) cm

4¾ (5, 5½)" / 12 (12.5, 14) cm

SHOULDER SEAMS

With *wrong sides facing* each other, and front of sweater facing you, place sts of back and front right shoulders on two parallel dpns. With a third dpn, k first stitch from front needle tog with first stitch from back needle, *k next stitch from front and back needles tog, sl first st over 2nd st to bind off; rep from * until all sts are bound off. Cut yarn and pull end through last loop.

SLEEVES

Mark for sleeves 4¾ (5 - 5¼)" / 12 (12.5 - 13.5) cm down from shoulder seam on front and back. With RS facing, pick up and k 52 (56 - 58) sts between markers. Work in St st for 5 rows, then dec 1 st each end on next row, then every 4th row 7 (6 - 8) times more, then every 2nd row 0 (3 - 1) times— 36 (36 - 38) sts. Work even until sleeve measures 5 (5.5 - 6)" / 12.5 (14 - 15.5) cm, end with a WS row. K 4 rows, then bind off loosely and evenly.

GARTER ST I-CORD TIES

Make 6. With dpn, cast on 3 sts. *Row 1 (RS):* K3. *Do not turn work. Slide sts to other end of needle to work next row from RS and p3; slide sts to other end of needle and k3; rep from * for 4" / 11.5 cm. Bind off.

FINISHING

Sew side and sleeve seams.

Neckband

With RS facing, pick up and k 52 (58 - 58) sts evenly around neck edge. P 1 row, k 1 row, p 1 row. Bind off.

Sew 3 ties evenly along left front edge. Overlap left front over right and sew rem 3 ties to right front so that ties line up. Knot ties together to close.

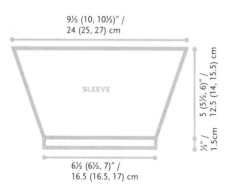

9½ (10, 10½)" / 24 (25, 27) cm

SLEEVE

5 (5½, 6)" / 12.5 (14, 15.5) cm

½" / 1.5cm

6½ (6½, 7)" / 16.5 (16.5, 17) cm

puff baby

bulky wool double-sided carriage blanket with bobbles • unisex • quickknit

Two blankets in different colors worked in a simple diamond pattern are sewn together to make a thick carriage robe. I-cord trims the edges, and bobbles adorn the front. Warm and toasty, a unique way to keep out the winter chill.

FINISHED SIZE

Approx 32″ × 36.5″ / 81.5 cm × 92.5 cm

MATERIALS

Bulky weight wool which will obtain gauge given below
950 yd. / 855 m color A
750 yd. / 675 m color B
Knitting needles, size 10.5 US (3 UK, 6.5 mm) or size needed to obtain gauge
Double pointed needles (dpns), size 10.5 US (3 UK, 6.5 mm)
Sample in photograph knit in Brown Sheep Bulky #M-110 Orange (A) and #M-105 Pink (B)

GAUGE

14 sts and 19 rows = 4″ / 10 cm over St st using size 10.5 US (3 UK, 6.5 mm) needles

14 sts and 22 rows = 4″ / 10 cm over chart pat using size 10.5 US (3 UK, 6.5 mm) needles
Always check gauge to save time and to ensure correct yardage and correct fit!

FRONT

With B, cast on 111 sts. Work in chart pat as foll: *Row 1 (RS):* K1 (selvage st), work 12-st rep of chart 9 times, work last st of chart, k1 (selvage st). Cont in pat as established, keeping first and last st in St st for selvage, until 12 rows of chart have been worked 16 times, then work rows 1–6 once more. Bind off.

BACK

With A, cast on 111 sts. Work in St st until same length as front. Bind off.

I-CORD EDGING

With two dpns and A, cast on 3 sts. *Row 1 (RS):* *K3, do not turn. Slide sts back to beg of needle to work next row from RS and k3. Rep from * for I-cord until it fits around outside edge of blanket. Do not bind off. With RS of front and back pieces facing, sew

Stitch key
□ St st
☒ Rev St st

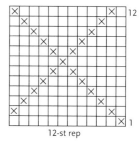

12-st rep

I-cord edging around outside edge of blanket, covering seams. Adjust length of I-cord if necessary, then bind off sts and sew ends together.

FINISHING

With A and dpns, work 272 bobbles as foll: Cast on 2 sts, leaving 2" / 5 cm tail. Slide sts to beg of needle, k in front and back of first st, k1, turn, p2tog, p1, turn, k2tog, cut yarn, leaving tail, and pull through. Tie ends tog to form bobble. With sewing needle, pull both ends of yarn through at intersections of diamond pat. Tie ends tog in knot on back of blanket. Trim ends evenly to about ½" / 1.5 cm long. *Note:* You can also make half the bobbles and place on every other intersection.

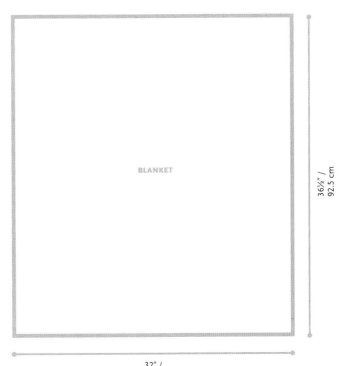

BLANKET

36½" /
92.5 cm

32" /
81.5 cm

baby bunting

bulky wool bunting with helmet • unisex

• super quickknit

There's nothing like a bunting to bring out the oohs and ahhs, and this outfit is no exception. Knit at 2.5 stitches to the inch, with enormous buttons, this bunting will be ready to bring baby home.

SIZES

Newborn (3 months - 6 months)
Finished chest: 28 (30 - 32)" / 71
(76 - 81.5) cm
Length, shoulder to foot: 17 (18 - 19)" / 43
(45.5 - 48.5) cm
Hat circumference (before I-cord border):
19" / 48.5 cm
Note: After I-cord border, finished
circumference is approx 3" / 7.5 cm smaller.

MATERIALS

Super bulky weight which will obtain gauge
given below
270 (300 - 350) yd. / 243 (270 - 315) m each
(A) and (B)
Knitting needles, size 13 US (00 UK, 9 mm)
or size needed to obtain gauge
Double pointed needles (dpns), size 13 US
(00 UK, 9 mm)
Crochet hook J
Stitch holders
Three 1½" /3.5 cm buttons

*Sample in photograph knit in Berroco Furz
#3801 White (A) and JCA / Reynolds Andean
Regal Alpaca #7 Blue (B)*

GAUGE

10 sts and 16 rows = 4" / 10 cm over St st
using size 13 (00 UK, 9 mm) needles
*Always check gauge to save time and to ensure
correct yardage and correct fit!*
Note: Work with 1 strand A and B held tog
throughout.

BUNTING

BACK

Right leg: Cast on 8 (7 - 8) sts. Beg with a
p row, work in St st, inc 1 st each side every
other row 4 (5 - 5) times—16 (17 - 18) sts.
Work even until piece measures 5½
(6 - 6½)" / 14 (15.5 - 16.5) cm from beg,
ending with a WS row. Place sts on holder.
Left leg: Work as for right leg.

JOIN LEGS

Next row (RS): With RS facing, k 16 (17 - 18)
sts of right leg, cast on 3 (3 - 4) sts (crotch),
k 16 (17 - 18) sts of left leg—35 (37 - 40) sts.
Work even until piece measures 11½
(12 - 12½)" / 29 (30.5 - 31.5) cm from
crotch, end WS row. **Shape neck:** *Next row
(RS):* Work 12 (13 - 14) sts for right shoulder
and place on holder for later finishing,
bind off center 11 (11 - 12) sts, work rem sts

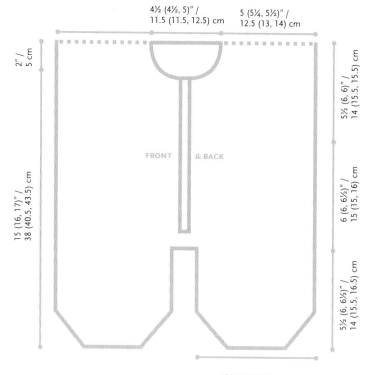

4½ (4½, 5)" /
11.5 (11.5, 12.5) cm

5 (5¼, 5½)" /
12.5 (13, 14) cm

2" /
5 cm

5½ (6, 6)" /
14 (15.5, 15.5) cm

FRONT & BACK

15 (16, 17)" /
38 (40.5, 43.5) cm

6 (6, 6½)" /
15 (15, 16) cm

5½ (6, 6½)" /
14 (15.5, 16.5) cm

6½ (7, 7¼)" /
16.5 (17.5, 18.5) cm

for left shoulder and place on holder for later finishing.

FRONT

Work same as back until 4 (6 - 8) rows have been worked above crotch.

DIVIDE FOR PLACKET

Next row (RS): K 19 (20 - 22) sts for left front, place rem 16 (17 - 18) sts on a holder for right front. Cont on left front sts only until piece measures 4″ / 10 cm above crotch, end WS. *Next row, buttonhole (RS):* Work to last 4 sts, bind off 2 sts, work to end. On next row, cast on 2 sts over bound-off sts. Work two more buttonholes 2″ / 5 cm apart. Work until piece measures 9½ (10 - 10½ - 11)″ / 24 (25.5 - 26.5) cm above crotch, end RS row. *Next row (WS):* Bind off 4 (4 - 5) sts from neck edge once, then dec 1 st every row 3 times. When same length as back, place rem 12 (13 - 14) sts on holder for later finishing. **Right front:** With RS facing, slip sts from holder to needle. Join yarn, cast on 3 (3 - 4) sts (buttonband), k across—19 (20 - 21) sts. Complete same as left front,

omitting buttonholes and reversing neck shaping. Overlap left front over right and stitch cast-on edge of buttonband in place.

SHOULDER SEAMS

With *wrong sides facing* each other, and front of bunting facing you, place sts of back and front right shoulders on two parallel dpns. With a third dpn, k first stitch from front needle tog with first stitch from back needle, *k next stitch from front and back needles tog, sl first st over 2nd st to bind off; rep from * until all sts are bound off. Cut yarn and pull end through last loop.

SLEEVES

Mark for sleeves 5½ (6 - 6)″ / 14 (15.5 - 15.5) cm down from shoulder seam on front and

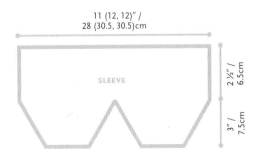

11 (12, 12)″ / 28 (30.5, 30.5)cm

SLEEVE

2½″ / 6.5cm

3″ / 7.5cm

back. With RS facing, pick up and k 28 (30 - 30) sts between markers. Work in St st for 3" / 7.5 cm, end WS row. **Shape hand:** *Next row (RS):* K2tog, k 10 (11 - 11), k2tog, join 2nd ball of yarn, k2tog, k 10 (11 - 11), k2tog. Working both sides at once, dec 1 st each end of each side 3 (4 - 4) times more. Place rem 6 (5 - 5) sts each side on a holder.

FINISHING

Sew side, leg, crotch, and sleeve seams, weaving (or knitting) tog open sts of hand. With crochet hook and 2 strands of yarn, work 1 row of sl st around front edge and collar. Sew on buttons.

HAT

HAT BODY

With 2 dpns and 1 strand A and B held tog, cast on 4 sts. Work I-cord as foll: *Row 1 (RS):*

k4. *Do not turn work. Slide sts to other end of needle to work next row from RS and k4; rep from * for 1" / 2.5 cm. Inc 1 st in each st on next row to 8 sts. Divide sts evenly over 4 dpns (2 sts on each needle). Join and work in rnds of St st (k every rnd), inc 1 st at end of every needle every rnd (therefore 4 sts inc every rnd) until there are 48 sts, or 12 sts on each needle. (*Note:* To make hat smaller or larger, work fewer or more rnds.) K 1 rnd, p 2 rnds. K every rnd for 2" / 5 cm, or desired length. Transfer sts to any size circular needle.

I-CORD BORDER

With 2 dpns, cast on 4 sts. With RS facing, work I-cord as before, attaching cord to lower edge of hat by knitting last st of I-cord tog with 1 st from circular needle through back loops. Bind off rem 4 sts and sew edges of I-cord edging together.

feltie feet

felted booties • felted bulky wool
• unisex • quickknit

The felted booties are a snap to knit and transform themselves into really wearable booties after two washings in the machine. Tie on a checkered bow, and voilà! An unbeatable welcome present when you're out of time.

SIZES

Newborn to 3 months
Length (after felting): 4″ / 10 cm.
Note: The finished size of the felted bootie can be affected by the type of yarn you are using as well as the temperature of water in your washing machine. The measurements here are consequently approximate, and it may take some experimentation to achieve the desired size.

MATERIALS

Following are approximate amounts based on using Brown Sheep Lamb's Pride Bulky yarn (#M180, Ruby Red). Other yarns and colors may felt more or less making a smaller or larger garment and thus may require different amounts of yarn to achieve the desired size.

Bulky yarn: 36 yd. / 32 m
Dpns, size 10.5 US (3 UK, 6.5 mm)
12″ / 30 cm, ¾″ / 2 cm ribbon

GAUGE

12 sts = 4″ / 10 cm over St st using size 10.5 US (3 UK, 6.5 mm) needles (before felting)
Always check gauge to save time and to ensure correct yardage and correct fit!

—————————————————————

M1 = make 1. Insert needle from behind under running st between last st worked and next st and place it on left-hand needle, then k into back of this loop.

—————————————————————

SOLE

With dpn, cast on 5 sts.
Row 1: K5. *Row 2:* P5. *Rnd 3:* K1, M1, k1, M1, k1, M1, k2 — 8 sts. *Rows 4 – 6:* Work in St st. *Row 7:* K2, k2tog, k1, k2tog, k1—6 sts. *Row 8:* P6. *Row 9:* K2, M1, k2, M1, k2—8 sts. *Row 10:* P8. *Row 11:* K3, M1, k2, M1, k3—10 sts. *Rows 12–14:* Work in St st. *Row 15:* K2, k2tog, k2, k2tog, k2—8 sts. *Row 16:* P8. *Row 17:* K1, k2tog, k2, k2tog, k1—6 sts.

Row 18: P6. *Row 19:* (K2tog) twice, *pull first st over 2nd to bind off. K2tog, rep from *. Sl rem st to dpn and with RS facing, pick up 25 sts around sole—26 sts. Join and k 3 rnds. Bind off knitwise, leaving 1 st on needle.

TONGUE

Pick up 1 st from bootie.
Next row: P2. *Next row:* K1, M1, k1. *Next row:* P3. *Next row:* K1, M1, k1, M1, k1—5 sts. *Next row:* P5. *Next row:* K1, M1, k1, M1, k1, M1, k2—8 sts. *Next 3 rows:* Work in St st. *Next row:* K2tog, k4, k2tog—6 sts. *Next row:* P6. *Next row:* K2tog, k2, k2tog—4 sts. *Next row:* P4. *Next row:* K2tog across, binding off at the same time. Cut yarn and pull end through loop. Sew edges of tongue to sides of bootie, and weave in all loose ends.

FELTING

In washing machine, set on hot wash/cold rinse, run though on small load for longest cycle 1 to 3 times, to desired size. Cut 2 6″ / 15 cm pieces of ribbon. Thread ribbon through top of tongue, tie in knot and trim.

welcome, baby

christening gown in a soft sport weight yarn
with bobbles and buttons • unisex

Reverse stocking knit edging and tiny poufs adorn this classic welcome outfit. Perfect for celebrations for either boys or girls.

SIZES

To fit 3 to 6 months
Finished chest: 16″ / 41 cm
Length from shoulder to hem: 25″ /
63.5 cm

MATERIALS

DK weight yarn that will obtain gauge
given below
Dress: 850 yd. / 765 m White (A)
Caplet: 140 yd. / 125 m White (A)
DK weight angora
Dress: 30 yd. / 27 m White (B)
Cap: 10 yd. / 9 m White (B)
20″ / 50 cm circular needle, size 4 US
(9 UK, 3.75 mm); 29″ / 72 cm circular size
6 US (7 UK, 4.5 mm) or size needed to
obtain gauge
Double pointed needles (dpns), sizes 4
and 6 US (9 and 7 UK, 3.5 and 4.5 mm)
Stitch holders and markers

*Sample in photograph knit in Rowan DK
Cotton #263 and Berroco Angora #9901*

GAUGE

20 sts and 28 rows = 4″ / 10 cm in St st
using size 6 needles
*Always check gauge to save time and to ensure
correct yardage and correct fit!*

GOWN

SKIRT

With larger circular needle and A, cast on 182 sts. Join, taking care not to twist st on needle and place marker for beg of rnd. *K 3 rnds, p 3 rnds; rep from * twice more. Cont

in St st (k every rnd) until piece measures 20½″ / 52 cm from beg.

BODICE

Next rnd: K2tog around—91 sts. Change to smaller circular needle and work in k1, p1 rib for 2 rnds, dec 1 st on first rnd—90 sts.

DIVIDE FOR FRONT AND BACK

Work 45 sts for front, place rem sts on a holder for back. Working back and forth on front sts only, cont in ribbing for 2¼″ / 5.5 cm. **Shape neck:** Work 19 sts, join 2nd ball of yarn and bind off center 7 sts for neck, work to end. Working both sides at same time, dec 1 st at each neck edge every other row 6 times, *at the same time,* when bodice measures 4″ / 10 cm, work buttonholes on left side of front as foll: *Next (buttonhole) row:* Rib 1, yo, k2tog, [rib 2, yo, k2tog] twice, rib to end. Work even until bodice measures 4.5″ / 11.5 cm. Bind off left shoulder sts and place 13 sts of right shoulder on a holder.

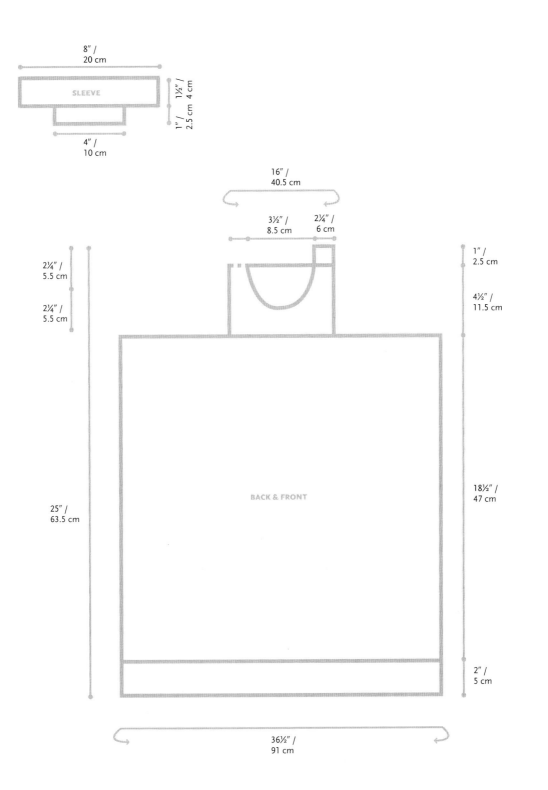

8" /
20 cm

SLEEVE

1½" /
4 cm

2.5 cm

1" /
2.5 cm

4" /
10 cm

16" /
40.5 cm

3½" /
8.5 cm

2¼" /
6 cm

2¼" /
5.5 cm

2¼" /
5.5 cm

1" /
2.5 cm

4½" /
11.5 cm

BACK & FRONT

18½" /
47 cm

25" /
63.5 cm

2" /
5 cm

36½" /
91 cm

BACK

Work as for front, omitting neck shaping and buttonholes, and working last row as foll: *Next row (RS):* Work 13 sts and place on a holder for right shoulder, bind off next 19 sts for neck, work to end. Cont on rem 13 sts in St st for left back button flap for 1" / 2.5 cm. Bind off.

RIGHT SHOULDER SEAM

With *wrong sides facing,* place sts of back and front right shoulders on two parallel size 4 dpns. With a third size 4 dpn, k through first st on each needle, then through the 2nd st on each needle, and pass first over 2nd to bind off. Cont in this way to end for a knitted seam. Pin left shoulder closed.

SLEEVES

Place markers on front and back 4" / 10 cm down from shoulder seams for armholes. With RS facing, size 6 dpns and A, pick up and k 40 sts between markers. Join and place marker at underarm. Work in St st (k every rnd) for 1½" / 4 cm. K2tog around—20 sts. Change to B and work in rev St st (p every rnd) for 1" / 2.5 cm. Bind off knitwise.

FINISHING

Collar

With RS facing, larger circular needles and B, beg at top of left front shoulder, pick up 48 sts evenly around neck edge. Work in rev St st for 1¼" / 3 cm. Bind off knitwise.

Bobbles: With size 6 needles and B, cast on 3 sts. *Row 1:* K1, k in front and back of next st, k1. *Row 2:* P4. *Row 3:* K1 [k in front and back of next st, k1], twice. *Row 4:* P6. *Row 5:* K3, k in front and back of next st, k t end. *Row 6:* *P2tog, p1; rep from * to end. *Row 7:* K1, k2tog, k1. *Row 8:* P2tog, p1. *Row 9:* K2tog. Cut yarn and form into a ball. Make 20 bobbles. Sew on 3 for buttons at shoulder

and sew rem evenly spaced along lower
ridge of skirt.

CAPLET

With larger size 2 dpns and B, cast on 4 sts.
Work I-cord as foll: *Row 1 (RS):* K4. *Do not
turn work. Slide sts to other end of needle to
work next row from RS and k4; rep from *
for 4 rows.

I-CORD TOPKNOT

Change to A. Inc 1 st in each st on next
row to 8 sts. Divide sts evenly over 4 dpns
(2 sts on each needle). Join and work in
rnds of St st (k every rnd), inc 1 st at end
of every needle every rnd (therefore 4 sts

inc'd every rnd) until there are 84 sts, or 21
sts on each needle. *Note:* To make hat
smaller or larger, work fewer or more rnds.
[P 4 rnds, k 4 rnds] twice. Transfer sts to
circular needle.

I-CORD BIND-OFF

With 2 dpns and B, cast on 4 sts. With RS
facing, work I-cord as before, attaching cord
to lower edge of hat by knitting last st of
I-cord tog with 1 st from circular needle
through back loops. Bind off rem 4 sts and
sew ends of I-cord together.

FINISHING

With B, make 6 bobbles and sew evenly
around brim of hat.

jeepers creepers
play clothes with dash and flair

Baby clothes are purely instant gratification for

any knitter, whether you have your own baby

or are knitting for another. These charmers are

quickknits, chic yet simple, with enchanting

details. And you just might be knitting

heirlooms . . . .

swing set

cotton swing top and diaper cover
* girls * quickknit

Swingy top in stripes is trimmed with a crocheted edging, and the diaper cover is simple garter stitch. Cute for the beach or summer days, in easy-care cotton.

SIZES

To fit 3 to 6 months (12–18 months - 2 Years)

Top

Finished chest: 19½ (21 - 23)″ / 49 (53 - 57) cm
Length, shoulder to hem: 12 (13 - 14½)″ / 30 (32.5 - 36.5) cm

Diaper Cover

Finished waist (buttoned): 14 (15 - 16)″ / 35.5 (37.5 - 40.5) cm
Length (unbuttoned): 12 (13 - 14)″ / 30.5 (33 - 35.5) cm

MATERIALS

Worsted weight cotton that will obtain gauge given below
Top: 165 (187 - 225) yd. / 150 (170 - 205) m each Cerise (A) and Flame (B)
Diaper cover: 85 (95 - 110) yd. / 77 (85 - 100) m Azure (C)
Knitting needles, straight sizes 4, 5, and 6 US (10, 9, 8 UK / 3.5, 3.75, and 4 mm) or size needed to obtain gauge
Double pointed needles (dpns), 6 US (8 UK / 4 mm)
Crochet hook size F US (9 UK or 4 mm)

1 yd. / 1 m ¾″ / 2 cm elastic
Two 1″ / 2.5 cm buttons for top, four buttons for diaper cover
Stitch holders
Sample in photograph knit in Rowan Handknit Cotton #233 (A), #254 (B), and #248 (C). If not available, substitute JCA / Reynolds Saucy #372 (A), #341 (B), and #640 (C).

GAUGE

Top: 20 sts and 28 rows = 4″ / 10 cm in St st using size 6 (8 UK / 4 mm) needles
Diaper cover: 20 sts and 36 rows = 4″ / 10 cm in seed st using size 5 (9 UK / 3.75 mm) needles
Always check gauge to save time and to ensure correct yardage and correct fit!

STRIPE PATTERN

Work 16 (18 - 20) rows each B, A, and B.

SEED STITCH

Row 1 (RS): *K1, p1; rep from * to end.
Row 2: K the purl sts and p the knit sts.
Rep row 2 for seed st.

TOP

FRONT

With largest needles and A, cast on 14
(16 - 18) sts. K 1 row. Working in garter st
(k all rows), cast on 3 sts beg of next 16
(18 - 18) rows, then 2 sts beg of next 2
(0 - 2) rows—66 (70 - 76) sts. K 1 row.
Starting with a RS row, work in stripe
pattern as foll: Work 7 sts garter st, 52 (56 -
62) sts in St st, 7 sts garter st, and *at the
same time*, dec 1 st each side every 18th
(20th - 16th) row 2 (2 - 3) times as foll:
On RS row, k7, k2tog, work to last 9 sts,
k2tog, k7—62 (66 - 70) sts rem. When
piece measures 6 (7 - 7½)" / 15 (17.5 - 19)
cm from beg of stripe pat, work
buttonholes as foll: K3, bind off 2 sts,
work to last 5 sts, bind off 2 sts, k to end.
On next row, cast on 2 sts over bound-off
sts. Work even completing stripe pat, end
WS row.

Shape armhole: With smallest size
needles and A and working in garter st,
bind off 3 sts at beg of next 2 rows, 2 sts
at beg of next 2 rows, dec 1 st each side
every other row 5 (6 - 6) times—42 (44 -
48) sts. Work even until armhole
measures 2¼ (2¼ - 2½)" / 5.5 (5.5 - 6.5)
cm, end WS row. Cut A. **Shape neck:** With
B, cont in garter st, work 16 (16 - 17) sts,
join 2nd ball of yarn and bind off center 10
(12 - 14) sts, work to end. Working both
sides at once, bind off from each neck
edge 2 sts twice, 1 st once. When armhole
measures 3 (3½ - 4)" / 7.5 (9 - 10) cm,
place rem 11 (11 - 12) sts each side on
holders for shoulders.

BACK

Work as for front, omitting
buttonholes.

FINISHING

Shoulder seams

With *wrong sides facing* each other, and front of garment facing you, place sts of back and front right shoulders on two parallel dpns. With a third dpn, k first stitch from front needle tog with first stitch from back needle, *k next stitch from front and back needles tog, sl first st over 2nd st to bind off; rep

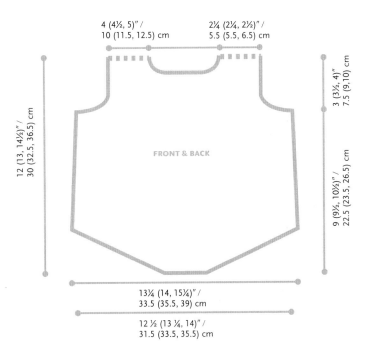

4 (4½, 5)" /
10 (11.5, 12.5) cm

2¼ (2¼, 2½)" /
5.5 (5.5, 6.5) cm

3 (3½, 4)" /
7.5 (9,10) cm

12 (13, 14½)" /
30 (32.5, 36.5) cm

FRONT & BACK

9 (9½, 10½)" /
22.5 (23.5, 26.5) cm

13¼ (14, 15¼)" /
33.5 (35.5, 39) cm

12 ½ (13 ¼, 14)" /
31.5 (33.5, 35.5) cm

from * until all sts are bound off. Cut yarn and pull end through last loop.

Sew buttons to RS of back opposite buttonholes. With crochet hook and B, work a row of seed st around neck and curve at lower edge of front and back as foll: *2 sc, 4 dc in next st; rep from * for seed st.

DIAPER COVER

BODY

With size 5 US (9 UK / 3.75 mm) needles and C, cast on 29 (31 - 33) sts. Work in seed st for 5½ (6 - 6½)" / 14 (15 - 16.5) cm. Place markers at side edges. Inc 1 st each side on next row, then every 4th row 5 (6 - 8) times more—41 (45 - 51) sts. Work even until piece measures 9 (10 - 11)" / 23 (25.5 - 28) cm from beg. Place markers at side edges. Inc 1 st each side every other row 3 times, cast on 2 sts beg of next 4 rows, 8 sts beg of next 2 rows—71 (75 - 81) sts. Work even for 1" / 2.5 cm. *Next row (buttonholes):* Work 5 sts, bind off 2 sts, work 3 sts, bind off 2, work to last 12 sts, bind off 2 sts, work 3 sts, bind off 2, work to end. On next row, cast on 2 sts over bound off sts. Work even until piece measures 12 (13 - 14)" / 30.5 (33 - 35.5) cm from beg. Bind off all sts.

FINISHING

Elastic casing: With RS facing, size 5 US (9 UK / 3.75 mm) needles and C, pick up and k 1 st in every other row between markers. K 1 row. *Next row (RS):* K. Cont in St st for 1" / 2.5 cm. Bind off. Fold casing to WS and sew in place, leaving an opening at each end for elastic. Thread elastic through casing and adjust to fit. Secure elastic and sew openings closed. Sew buttons on front flap, opposite buttonholes.

seedling

worsted cardigan with big buttons

· unisex · quickknit

A cardigan for all seasons and sexes, in simple seed stitch. Big buttons close the front, making a colorful embellishment. Manos del Uruguay hand-dyed wool has a soft color variation that gives the seed stitch fabric a subtle patterning.

SIZES

3 to 6 months (1 year - 2 years - 3 years)
Finished chest (buttoned): 20
(23 - 25 - 27)" / 51 (58.5 - 63.5 - 68.5) cm
Length, shoulder to hem: 10 (12 - 13 - 14)" /
25 (30.5 - 33 - 35.5) cm

MATERIALS

Heavy worsted weight yarn which will obtain
gauge given below
250 (300 - 360 - 420) yd. /230
(275 - 330 - 385) m
Knitting needles, size 8 US (6 UK, 5 mm) or
size needed to obtain gauge
Double pointed needles (dpns) size 8 US
(6 UK, 5 mm)
Stitch holders and markers
Three (4 - 4 - 5) ½" / 1.5 cm buttons
*Sample in photograph knit in Manos del
Uruguay in #47 Fuchsia*

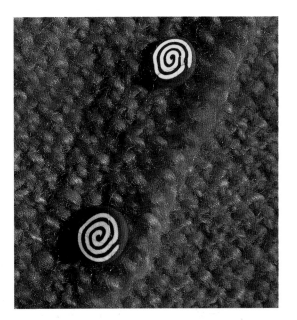

GAUGE

16 sts and 32 rows = 4" / 10 cm over seed st
using size 8 US (6 UK, 5 mm) needles
*Always check gauge to save time and to ensure
correct yardage and correct fit!*

SEED STITCH

Row 1 (RS): *K1, p1; rep from * to end.
Row 2: K the purl sts and p the knit sts.
Rep row 2 for seed st.

BACK

Cast on 40 (46 - 50 - 54) sts. Work in seed st until piece measures 10 (12 - 13 - 14)" / 25 (30.5 - 33 - 35.5) cm from beg, end with a WS row. Work 13 (15 - 17 - 18) sts and place on a holder for right shoulder, bind off next 14 (16 - 16 - 18) sts for back neck, work rem sts and place on a 2nd holder for left shoulder.

LEFT FRONT

Cast on 22 (25 - 27 - 29) sts. Work in seed st until piece measures 8½" (10½ - 11½ - 12½)" / 21 (26.5 - 29 - 31.5) cm from beg, end with a RS row. **Shape neck:** *Next row (WS):* Bind off 3 (4 - 4 - 5) sts (neck edge), work to end. Cont to bind off from neck edge 2 sts 3 times. When same length as back, place rem 13 (15 - 17 - 18) sts on a holder for later finishing. Place markers on band for 3 (4 - 4 - 5) buttons, the first ½" / 1.5 cm below neck edge and the others spaced 2¼" (2½ - 2¾ - 2½)" / 5.5 (6.5 - 7 - 6.5) cm apart.

RIGHT FRONT

Work to correspond to left front, reversing neck shaping, and working buttonholes opposite markers as foll: *Buttonhole row (RS):* Work 2 sts, yo, k2tog, work to end.

SHOULDER SEAMS

With *wrong sides facing* each other, and front of sweater facing you, place sts of back and front right shoulders on two parallel dpns. With a third dpn, k first stitch from front needle tog with first stitch from back needle,

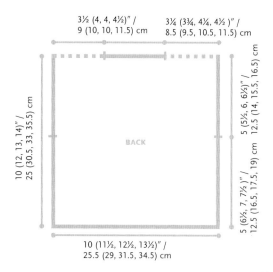

3½ (4, 4, 4½)" /
9 (10, 10, 11.5) cm

3¼ (3¾, 4¼, 4½)" /
8.5 (9.5, 10.5, 11.5) cm

10 (12, 13, 14)" /
25 (30.5, 33, 35.5) cm

BACK

5 (5½, 6, 6½)" /
12.5 (14, 15.5, 16.5) cm

5 (6½, 7, 7½)" /
12.5 (16.5, 17.5, 19) cm

10 (11½, 12½, 13½)" /
25.5 (29, 31.5, 34.5) cm

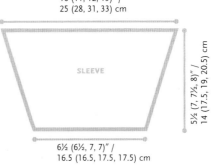

*k next stitch from front and back needles tog, sl first st over 2nd st to bind off; rep from * until all sts are bound off. Cut yarn and pull end through last loop.

SLEEVES

Mark for sleeves 5 (5½ - 6 - 6½)" / 12.5 (14 - 15.5 - 16.5) cm down from shoulder seam on front and back. With RS facing, pick up and k 40 (44 - 48 - 52) sts between markers. Work in seed st for 3 rows, then dec 1 st each end (working dec sts into seed st) on next row, then every 6th row 6 (8 - 8 - 6) times more, every 4th row 0 (0 - 1 - 5) times—26 (26 - 28 - 28) sts. Work even until sleeve measures 5½

(7 - 7½ - 8)" / 14 (17.5 - 19 - 20.5) cm, end with a WS row. Bind off loosely and evenly.

FINISHING

Sew side and sleeve seams.

Neckband

With RS facing, pick up and k 50 (54 - 54 - 58) sts evenly around neck edge. Work in seed st for 3 rows. Bind off.
   Sew on buttons.

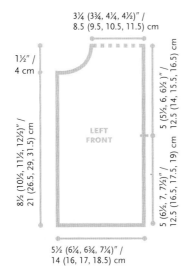

3¼ (3¾, 4¼, 4½)" / 8.5 (9.5, 10.5, 11.5) cm

1½" / 4 cm

8½ (10¼, 11½, 12½)" / 21 (26.5, 29, 31.5) cm

LEFT FRONT

5 (5½, 6, 6½)" / 12.5 (14, 15.5, 16.5) cm

5 (6½, 7, 7½)" / 12.5 (16.5, 17.5, 19) cm

5½ (6¼, 6¾, 7¼)" / 14 (16, 17, 18.5) cm

10 (11, 12, 13)" / 25 (28, 31, 33) cm

SLEEVE

5½ (7, 7½, 8)" / 14 (17.5, 19, 20.5) cm

6½ (6½, 7, 7)" / 16.5 (16.5, 17.5, 17.5) cm

flax jax

worsted cardigan • unisex • quickknit

This wool cardi knits up quickly in worsted yarn, with seed stitch stripes around the back. Pure off-white yarn makes a simple statement, with seed stitch details and charming collar.

SIZES

To fit 3 to 6 months (1 year - 2 years - 3 years)
Finished chest (buttoned): 19 (23 - 25 - 27)" / 48.5 (58.5 - 63.5 - 68.5) cm
Length, shoulder to hem: 9 (11 - 12 - 13)" / 22.5 (28 - 31 - 33) cm

MATERIALS

Heavy worsted weight yarn which will obtain gauge given below
400 (570 - 670 - 790) yd. / 360 (513 - 603 - 710) m
Knitting needles, size 9 US (5 UK, 5.5 mm) or size needed to obtain gauge
Double pointed needles (dpns), size 9 US (5 UK, 5.5 mm)
Stitch holders and markers
Three (3 - 4 - 4) 1" / 2.5 cm buttons
Sample in photograph knit in Brown Sheep Lambs Pride Worsted in #M-11 White Frost

GAUGE

16 sts and 24 rows = 4" / 10 cm over St st using size 9 US (5 UK, 5.5 mm) needles
Always check gauge to save time and to ensure correct yardage and correct fit!
Note: Body is worked in one piece to the underarm.

SEED STITCH

Row 1 (RS): *K1, p1; rep from * to end.
Row 2: K the purl sts and p the knit sts.
Rep row 2 for seed st.

STRIPE PATTERN

*6 rows St st, 6 rows seed st; rep from
* (12 rows) for stripe pat.

BODY

With MC, cast on 80 (96 - 104 - 112) sts.
Work in seed st for 1″ / 2.5 cm, end with a
WS row. *Next row (RS):* Work 4 sts in seed
st, work 12 (16 - 17 - 19) sts in St st, place
marker, work 48 (56 - 62 - 66) sts in stripe
pat, place marker, work 12 (16 - 17 - 19) sts
in St st, work 4 sts in seed st. Cont in pat as
established until piece measures 2½
(2¾ - 2¼ - 2½)″ / 6.5 (7 - 5.5 - 6.5) cm from
beg, end with a WS row. *Buttonhole row (RS):*
Work 2 sts, yo, p2tog, work to end. Rep
buttonhole row every 2½ (2¾ - 2¼ - 2½)″ /
6.5 (7 - 5.5 - 6.5) cm 2 (2 - 3 - 3) times more,
and *at the same time,* when piece measures

4 (5½ - 6 - 6½)″ / 10 (14 - 15.5 - 16.5) cm
from beg, end with a WS row. Remove
markers.

DIVIDE FOR FRONTS AND BACK

Next row (RS): Work seed st band and 17
(21 - 23 - 25) sts in St st and place on a
holder for right front, cont in stripe pat over
next 38 (46 - 50 - 54) sts for back, place rem
21 (25 - 27 - 29) sts on a holder for left front.
Cont in stripe pat on back sts only until
piece measures 9 (11 - 12 - 13)″ / 22.5
(28 - 31 - 33) cm from beg, end WS row.
Work 11 (14 - 16 - 17) sts and place on a
holder for right shoulder, bind off next 16
(18 - 18 - 20) sts for neck, work rem sts on a
2nd holder for left shoulder.

LEFT FRONT

Work 21 (25 - 27 - 29) sts from left front
holder and cont in St st and seed st band
until piece measures 7½ (9½ - 10½ - 11½)″
/ 18.5 (24 - 27 - 29) cm from beg, end with a
WS row. **Shape neck:** *Next row (RS):* Work to
last 4 sts, place 4 sts on a holder. *Next row:*
Bind off 2 (3 - 3 - 4) sts (neck edge), work to

end. Cont to bind off from neck edge 2 sts twice. When same length as back, place rem 11 (14 - 16 - 17) sts on a holder for later finishing.

RIGHT FRONT

Work to correspond to left front, working buttonholes as established and reversing neck shaping.

SHOULDER SEAMS

With *wrong sides facing* each other, and front of sweater facing you, place sts of back and front right shoulders on two parallel dpns. With a third dpn, k first stitch from front needle tog with first stitch from back needle, *k next stitch from front and back needles tog, sl first st over 2nd st to bind off; rep from * until all sts are bound off. Cut yarn and pull end through last loop.

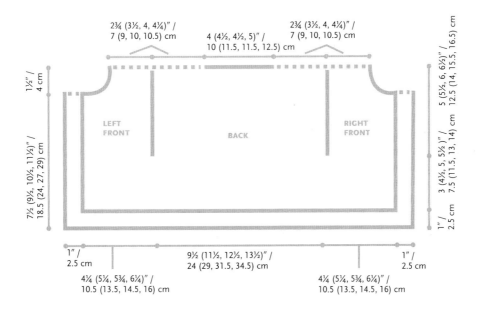

2¾ (3½, 4, 4¼)" / 7 (9, 10, 10.5) cm

4 (4½, 4½, 5)" / 10 (11.5, 11.5, 12.5) cm

2¾ (3½, 4, 4¼)" / 7 (9, 10, 10.5) cm

1½" / 4 cm

5 (5½, 6, 6½)" / 12.5 (14, 15.5, 16.5) cm

LEFT FRONT

BACK

RIGHT FRONT

7½ (9½, 10½, 11½)" / 18.5 (24, 27, 29) cm

3 (4½, 5, 5½)" / 7.5 (11.5, 13, 14) cm

1" / 2.5 cm

1" / 2.5 cm

9½ (11½, 12½, 13½)" / 24 (29, 31.5, 34.5) cm

1" / 2.5 cm

4¼ (5¼, 5¾, 6¼)" / 10.5 (13.5, 14.5, 16) cm

4¼ (5¼, 5¾, 6¼)" / 10.5 (13.5, 14.5, 16) cm

SLEEVES

With RS facing and dpns, pick up and k 40 (44 - 48 - 52) sts around armhole. Join, place marker, and k 5 (7 - 5 - 5) rnds, then dec 1 st before and after marker on next rnd, then every 4th rnd 6 (7 - 9 - 10) times—26 (28 - 28 - 30) sts. Work even until sleeve measures 5½ (6¾ - 7¼ - 8)" / 14 (17 - 18.5 - 20.5) cm. Work in seed st for ½" / 1.5 cm. Bind off loosely and evenly.

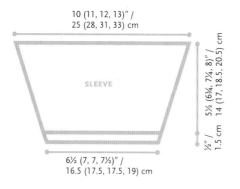

10 (11, 12, 13)" /
25 (28, 31, 33) cm

SLEEVE

5½ (6¾, 7¼, 8)" /
14 (17, 18.5, 20.5) cm

½" /
1.5 cm

6½ (7, 7, 7½)" /
16.5 (17.5, 17.5, 19) cm

FINISHING

Collar

With RS facing, cont in seed st, work 4 sts of buttonhole band, pick up and k 32 (36 - 36 - 40) sts evenly around neck edge, work 4 sts from buttonband in seed st—40 (44 - 44 - 48) sts. Work in seed st for 5 rows. *Next row (RS):* Work 2 sts seed st, *work double inc as foll: [k and p into each of next 2 sts], work 6 (7 - 7 - 8) sts seed st, work double inc; work 7 (8 - 8 - 9) sts seed st; rep from * once more, work double inc, work last 2 sts seed st—50 (54 - 54 - 58) sts. Work 3 rows even. *Next row (RS):* Work 2 sts seed st, work double inc, work seed st to last 4 sts, work double inc, work last 2 sts seed st—54 (58 - 58 - 62) sts. Cont in seed st for 5 rows more. Bind off knitwise.

Sew on buttons.

cable-alls

worsted wool cardigan, overalls, and cap
with cables • unisex • quickknit

All-over cables make this ensemble a warm outfit for babies and toddlers. Sporting a tasseled top, the cap has a roller brim. High-waisted overalls have leg buttons for easy dressing and changes, and the sweater is a classic. Perfect for boys or girls.

SIZES

To fit newborn to 3 (6–12 months - 18–24 months)

Cardigan

Finished chest (buttoned): 19½ (22½ - 25½)" / 49.5 (57 - 64.5) cm
Length, shoulder to hem: 9 (10½ - 12)" / 22.5 (26.5 - 30.5) cm

Overalls

Finished chest (buttoned): 19 (22 - 25)" / 48.5 (56 - 63.5) cm
Length (without straps): 13½ (14½ - 16)" / 34 (36.5 - 40) cm

Hat

Finished head circumference: 16 (18 - 20)" / 40 (45 - 50) cm

MATERIALS

Heavy worsted weight wool which will obtain gauge given below
Cardigan: 285 (345 - 415) yd. / 260 (315 - 380) m
Overalls: 345 (415 - 485) yd. / 315 (380 - 445) m
Hat: 75 (85 - 95) yd. / 70 (80 - 90) m (small amt of CC for tassel)

Knitting needles, size 9 US (5 UK, 5.5 mm) or size needed to obtain gauge
Overalls: 20" circular needle, size 9 US (5 UK, 5.5 mm)
Double pointed needles (dpns), size 9 US (5 UK, 5.5 mm)
Stitch holders and markers
Cable needle
Cardigan: Four ¾" / 2 cm buttons
Overalls: Six ¾" / 2 cm buttons
Sample in photograph knit in Manos del Uruguay in #05 Aqua

GAUGE

24 sts and 24 rows = 4" / 10 cm over cable pat using size 9 US (5 UK, 5.5 mm) needles
Always check gauge to save time and to ensure correct yardage and correct fit!

CABLE PATTERN

(multiple of 9 sts plus 3 extra)

Row 1 (RS): P3, *k6, p3; rep from *

Row 2 and all WS rows: K the knit sts and p the purl sts.

Row 3: P3, *sl 3 sts to cn and hold to back of work, k3, k3 from cn, p3; rep from *.

Rows 5 and 7: Rep row 1.

Row 8: Rep row 2.

Rep rows 1–8 for cable pat.

CARDIGAN

BACK

Cast on 57 (66 - 75) sts. Work in k1, p1 rib for ½" / 1.5 cm. Work in cable pat until piece measures 9 (10½ - 12)" / 22.5 (26.5 - 30.5) cm from beg, end with a WS row. Work 18 (21 - 25) sts and place on a holder for right shoulder, bind off next 21 (24 - 25) sts for back neck, work rem sts and place on a 2nd holder for left shoulder.

LEFT FRONT

Cast on 32 (36 - 41) sts. *Next row (RS):* Work in k1, p1 rib to last 4 sts, work last 4 sts in garter st (for button band). Cont as established for ½" / 1.5 cm, end with a WS row. **Beg cable pat:** *Next row (RS):* P3 (4 - 3), [k6, p3] 2 (2 - 3) times, k6, p1 (4 - 1), cont last 4 sts in garter st. Cont in pat as established until piece measures 7½ (9 - 10½)" / 18.5 (23 - 26.5) cm from beg, end with a RS row. **Shape neck:** *Next row (WS):* Work 4 sts and place on a holder, bind off 4 (5 - 6) sts (neck edge), work to end. Cont to bind off from neck edge 2 sts 3 times. When same length as back, place rem 18 (21 - 25) sts on a holder for later finishing. Place markers on garter st band for 3 buttons, ½" / 1.5 cm from top and bottom edges and the last spaced evenly between.

RIGHT FRONT

Work to correspond to left front, beg cable pat as foll: *Next row (RS):* Work 4 sts in garter st, p1 (4 - 1), [k6, p3] 2 (2 - 3) times, k6, p3 (4 - 3). Cont to work pats as established, working buttonholes opposite markers on RS row as foll: K2, k2tog, yo, work to end. Complete as for left front, reversing neck shaping.

SLEEVES

Mark for sleeves 5 (5½ - 5½)" / 12.5 (14 - 14) cm down from shoulder seam on front and back. With RS facing, pick up and k 57 (66 - 66) sts between markers. Work in cable pat for 5 rows, then dec 1 st each end (working dec sts into cable pat) on next row, then every 4th row 4 (2 - 3) times more, every 2nd row 4 (10 - 9) times— 39 (40 - 40) sts. Work even until sleeve measures 5½ (6 - 6½)" / 14 (15.5 - 16.5) cm. Work in k1, p1 rib for ½" / 1.5 cm. Bind off loosely and evenly in rib.

FINISHING

Sew side and sleeve seams.

Neckband

With RS facing, pick up and k 52 (58 - 58) sts evenly around neck edge, including sts from neck holders. K 3 rows. Bind off knitwise. Sew on buttons.

SHOULDER SEAMS

With *wrong sides facing* each other, and front of sweater facing you, place sts of back and front right shoulders on two parallel dpns. With a third dpn, k first stitch from front needle tog with first stitch from back needle, *k next stitch from front and back needles tog, sl first st over 2nd st to bind off; rep from * until all sts are bound off.

OVERALLS

LEFT LEG

Cast on 36 (42 - 50) sts. Work in garter st for ½" / 1.5 cm, inc 3 (6 - 7) sts evenly across last row—39 (48 - 57) sts. *Next row (RS):* [P3, k6] 4 (5 - 6) times, p3. Cont in cable pat as established, inc 1 st each side (working inc sts in St st) every 6th row 4 times—47 (56 - 65) sts. Work even until piece measures 6 (6½ - 7)" / 15.5 (16.5 - 17.5) cm from beg. Place sts on a holder.

RIGHT LEG

Work same as right leg. Leave sts on needle.

JOIN LEGS

Next row (RS:) With circular needle, work 47 (56 - 65) sts of right leg, cast on 7 sts, work 47 (56 - 65) sts of left leg, cast on 7 sts—108 (126 - 144) sts. Join, place marker, and cont in cable pat for 1 (1 - 1½)" / 2.5 (2.5 - 4) cm.

Shape placket: *Next row:* Cast on 4 sts, then k these 4 sts (buttonhole band), cont to work cable pat to last 3 sts, inc 1, k 3—113

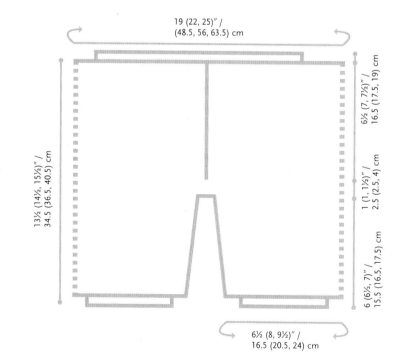

19 (22, 25)" /
(48.5, 56, 63.5) cm

13½ (14½, 15½)" /
34.5 (36.5, 40.5) cm

6½ (7, 7½)" /
16.5 (17.5, 19) cm

1 (1, 1½)" /
2.5 (2.5, 4) cm

6 (6½, 7)" /
15.5 (16.5, 17.5) cm

6½ (8, 9½)" /
16.5 (20.5, 24) cm

(131 - 149) sts. Work back and forth, cont to k first and last 4 sts in garter st until placket measures ½" / 1.5 cm, end WS row. *Next row, buttonhole (RS):* K2, yo, k2tog, work to end. Work 3 more buttonholes every 1½ (1¾ - 2)" / 4 (4.5 - 5) cm. Work even until placket measures 6½ (7 - 7½)" / 16.5 (17.5 - 19) cm, end WS row. *Next row (RS):* [K1, k2tog] 37 (43 - 49) times, k2—76 (88 - 100) sts. K 1 row. Work buttonhole beg of next row. K 1 more row. Bind off. Overlap bands and sew cast on edge of buttonhole band in place.

STRAPS

Cast on 8 sts. P1, work cable on 6 sts, p1. Cont in cable pat with the first and last st in rev St st until piece measures 10 (10 - 11)" / 25.5 (25.5 - 28) cm, or desired length. Bind off. Sew straps to front and back, sewing a button in center of each front strap.

FINISHING

Knitted buttons (make 7): Cast on 2 sts leaving long end. K1, inc 1—3 sts. *Next row:* P2tog, p1. *Next row:* K2tog. Cut yarn leaving long end and pull through rem st. Tie ends together to form button.

Back leg edging, buttonband: With back of garment and RS of knitting facing you and straight needles, pick up 48 (54 - 60) sts along inseam of left leg, crotch and right leg. K 7 rows. Bind off.

Front leg edging, buttonhole band: Pick up sts along front edges of legs and crotch as for back. K 3 rows. *Next row, buttonholes (RS):* K2, [k2tog, yo, k5 (6 - 7)] 6 times, k2tog, yo, k2. K 3 rows. Bind off loosely and evenly.

Sew knitted buttons to buttonband opposite buttonholes.

HAT

With straight needles, cast on 72 (81 - 90) sts. Work in St st starting with a WS row for 5 rows. Work in cable pat until piece measures 6 (6½ - 7)" / 15 (16 - 17.5) cm, end WS row. **Shape crown:** *K2 tog, k1; rep from * across— 48 (54 - 60) sts. *Next RS row:* *K2 tog across— 24 (27 - 30) sts. *Next RS row:* *K2 tog across, end k 0 (1 - 0)—12 (14 - 15) sts. *Next row:* P2 tog across, end p 0 (0 - 1)—6 (7 - 8) sts. Cut yarn, leaving long end. Pull end through loops and sew back seam, working seam on RS for last 1" / 2.5 cm so that it's invisible when brim rolls up. With CC, make 3" / 7.5 cm very full tassel and attach to top of hat.

dutch treat

pullover and trousers with pleats and ties
• unisex • sport weight wool

For the more adventurous knitter, this two-piece outfit has it all: bird's-eye in Fair Isle, colorblocked inverted pant pleats, I-cord ties, and color galore. For boys or girls, a celebratory ensemble with stylish wit.

SIZES

To fit 6 (12 - 18) months

SWEATER

Finished chest: 19 (22 - 24)" / 49 (56 - 61) cm
Length, shoulder to hem: 10 (11 - 12)" / 25 (28 - 30.5) cm

PANTS

Finished width (at widest part): 20 (24 - 24)"
Length: 12½ (13¼ - 14)" / 31 (33 - 35) cm

MATERIALS

Worsted weight yarn which will obtain gauge given below
Sweater: 300 (380 - 455) yd. / 275 (345 - 415) m (MC)
30 (35 - 40) yd. / 28 (32 - 36) m (A)
Pants: 250 (320 - 340) yd. / 230 (295 - 310) m (MC)
35 (45 - 50) yd. / 32 (42 - 46) m (A)
75 (80 - 85) yd. / 70 (75 - 80) m (B)
Knitting needles, straight sizes 6 US (8 UK, 4 mm) and 7 US (7 UK, 4.5 mm)
Pants: 29" circular needle, size 7 US (7 UK, 4.5 mm)

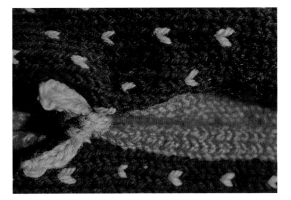

Double pointed needles (dpns), size 6 US (8 UK, 4 mm)
Stitch holders and markers
Sweater: two ½" / 1.5 cm buttons
Pants: six ½" / 1.5 cm buttons
Pants: 18" / 45 cm piece of ½" / 1 cm flat elastic
Sample in photograph knit in Brown Sheep Nature Spun in Purple #N65 (MC), Turquoise #N78 (A) and Orange #861 (B)

GAUGE

20 sts and 24 rows = 4" / 10 cm over St st using size 7 US (7 UK, 4.5 mm) needles
Always check gauge to save time and to ensure correct yardage and correct fit!

Color key

Color key
☐ MC
☒ A

6-st rep

PULLOVER

BACK

With smaller needles and MC, cast on 48 (54 - 60) sts. Starting with a p row, work in St st for 5 rows. *Next row (RS):* P. Cont in St st for 5 more rows. Change to larger needles and work chart until piece measures 10 (11 - 12)″ / 25 (28 - 30.5) cm from beg, end with a WS row. *Next row (RS):* K 13 (16 - 18) sts and place on a holder for right shoulder, bind off next 22 (22 - 24) sts for neck, p rem 13 (16 - 18) sts for left shoulder. **Button flap:** *Next row (WS):* P. Cont in St st for 1″ / 2.5 cm. Bind off.

FRONT

Work same as back until piece measures 8½ (9½ - 10½)″ / 21 (24 - 26.5) cm from beg, end with a WS row. **Shape neck:** *Next row (RS):* Work 18 (21 - 23) sts, join 2nd ball of yarn and bind off center 12 (12 - 14) sts, work to end. Working both sides at the same time, cont to bind off from each neck edge 3 sts once, dec 1 st every other row twice, and *at the same time,* when piece measures 9½ (10½ - 11½)″ / 23.5 (26.5 - 29) cm from beg, work buttonholes on left shoulder as foll: *Next row (RS):* K3 (4 - 5), k2tog, yo, k4, k2tog, yo, k to end. When same length as back, bind off 13 (16 - 18) left shoulder sts and place 13 (16 - 18) right shoulder sts on a holder for later finishing.

SHOULDER SEAMS

With *wrong sides facing* each other, and front of sweater facing you, place sts of back and front right shoulders on two parallel dpns. With a third dpn, k first stitch from front needle tog with first stitch from back needle, *k next stitch from front and back needles tog, sl first st over 2nd st to bind off; rep from * until all sts are bound off. Cut yarn and pull end through last loop.

NECKBAND

With smaller needle and MC, RS facing, pick up and k 62 (66 - 66) sts evenly around neck edge, including side of button flap. Work back and forth in St st for 1" / 2.5 cm. Bind off loosely.

Sew buttons to left shoulder.

SLEEVES

Mark for sleeves 5 (5½ - 5½)" / 12.5 (14 - 14) cm down from shoulder seam on front and back. With RS facing and MC, pick up and k 50 (56 - 56) sts between markers (working through all thicknesses on left side). Starting with a p row, work 3 rows St st, then work first 2 rows of chart as foll: K1, work chart on next 48 (54 - 54) sts, k1. Cont to work chart as established, dec 1 st each end on next row, then every 4th row 3 (6 - 6) times more, then every 2nd row 4 (3 - 2) times—34 (36 - 38) sts. *At the same time*, when sleeve

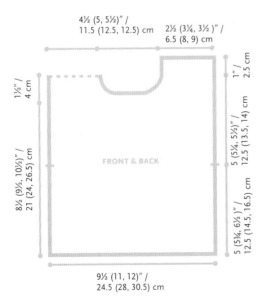

4½ (5, 5½)" / 11.5 (12.5, 12.5) cm
2½ (3¼, 3½)" / 6.5 (8, 9) cm
1½" / 4 cm
1" / 2.5 cm
5 (5¼, 5½)" / 12.5 (13.5, 14) cm
FRONT & BACK
8½ (9½, 10½)" / 21 (24, 26.5) cm
5 (5¾, 6½)" / 12.5 (14.5, 16.5) cm
9½ (11, 12)" / 24.5 (28, 30.5) cm

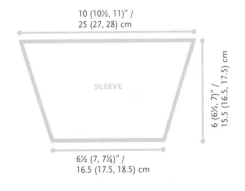

10 (10½, 11)" / 25 (27, 28) cm
SLEEVE
6 (6½, 7)" / 15.5 (16.5, 17.5) cm
6½ (7, 7¼)" / 16.5 (17.5, 18.5) cm

measures 5½ (6 - 6½)" / 14 (15 - 16) cm, end WS row. Cut A and cont with MC and St st for 4 rows. *Next row (RS):* P. Change to smaller needles and work 5 more rows St st. Bind off loosely and evenly.

FINISHING

Sew side and sleeve seams.

PANTS

RIGHT LEG

With circular needle and MC, cast on 66 (78 - 78) sts. Work back and forth as foll: *Rows 1 and 3 (WS):* K4, p to last 4 sts, k4. *Row 2:* K. *Next row:* With MC, k4, work St st and chart on next 18 (24 - 24) sts, work 1 st rev St st; with B, work 20 sts St st (pleat); with MC, work 1 st rev St st, work St st and chart on next 18 (24 - 24) sts, k4. Cont to work sts as established, inc 1 st each edge every 6th row 6 times as foll: K4, inc, work to last 4 sts, inc, k4— 78 (90 - 90) sts.

At the same time, work buttonhole every 2 (2½ - 3)" / 5 (6 - 7.5) cm twice as foll: On RS row, k3, yo, k2tog, work rem sts. Work even until piece measures 6 (6½ - 7)" / 15 (16 - 17.5) cm, end WS row. Bind off 2 sts beg of next 2 rows, then dec 1 st each end every other row twice—70 (82 - 82) sts, end with WS row. Place sts on holder.

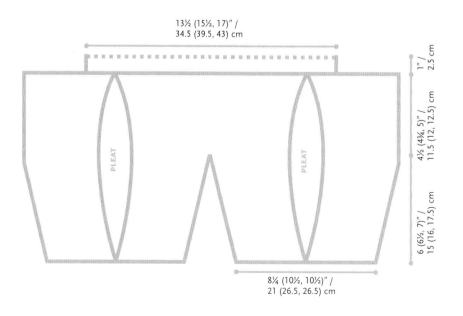

13½ (15½, 17)" / 34.5 (39.5, 43) cm

PLEAT

PLEAT

1" / 2.5 cm

4½ (4¾, 5)" / 11.5 (12, 12.5) cm

6 (6½, 7)" / 15 (16, 17.5) cm

8¼ (10½, 10½)" / 21 (26.5, 26.5) cm

LEFT LEG

Work same as left leg working buttonholes as foll: On RS row, work to last 5 sts, k2tog, yo, k3. When complete, leave sts on needle.

JOIN LEGS

RS row: Keeping to pat, work sts on needle, work sts from holder—140 (164 - 164) sts. Cont to work back and forth on sts as established—24 (30 - 30) sts in chart (½ of back), 1 st rev St st, 20 sts B (pleat), 1 st rev St st, 48 (60 - 60) sts in chart (front), 1 st rev St st, 20 sts B (pleat), 1 st rev St st, 24 (30 - 30) sts in chart (½ of back)—until piece measures 4½ (4¾ - 5)″ / 11.5 (12 - 12.5) cm from crotch, end WS row. **Waistband:** *Next row (RS):* [K2, k2tog] 6 (7 - 7) times, k 1 (3 - 3), bind off 20 sts of pleat, [k2, k2tog] 12 (15 - 15) times, k2tog, bind off 20 sts of pleat, k1, [k2, k2tog] 6 (7 - 7) times, k0 (2 - 2)—75 (94 - 94) sts. P 1 row. Dec 0 (9 - 0) sts evenly across next row—75 (85 - 94) sts. Work 2 more rows St st. *Next row, turning ridge (WS):* K. Cont in St st for 5 more rows. Bind off.

FINISHING

Sew back seam. Fold waistband to inside at turning ridge, inserting elastic, and sew in

place. Adjust elastic to size and sew opening closed. Fold pleat to inside so that MC edges meet in front. On WS sew pleat to bottom edge of waistband through both layers.

LEG CUFFS

Fold pleat to inside as for waist and pin in place. With smaller needles and MC, pick up and k 46 (50 - 52) sts evenly along lower edge of each leg, working through all thicknesses of pleat. Work in k1, p1 rib for ½″ / 1 cm. Work buttonhole at front edge. Work in rib for another ½″ / 1 cm. Bind off in rib.

I-CORD TIES (make 8)

With dpn and A, cast on 3 sts. *Row 1 (RS):* K3, *do not turn work. Slide sts to other end of needle to work next row from RS and k3; rep from * for 3″ / 7.5 cm. Bind off. Attach 4 ties to each leg at either side of pleat and tie tog. Sew on buttons.

brrrr...
warm wonders for crispy days

Bundling babies for an outdoor walk is a

delightful challenge with all the new

sumptuous yarns available now. Playful

silhouettes and unusual constructions in this

mini collection are easy to knit or felt. Hand-

knit garments are always a wonderful way to

keep your baby cozy and warm, and bulky

cold-weather wear knits up in a snap!

With a definite style of its own, this charming hat has earflaps adorned with pom-poms. Striped and knit from the top down, this cap is a showstopper!

To fit newborn to 6 months (12 months - 18 months)
Finished head circumference: 15 (17 - 19)" / 40 (45 - 50) cm

Bulky weight yarn that will obtain gauge given below
60 (70 - 80) yd. / 55 (65 - 75) m (MC)
1 (1 - 1) yd. (A)
20 (25 - 30) yd. / 15 (20 - 25) m (B)
Knitting needles, double pointed needles (dpns), size 10 US (4 UK, 6 mm) or size needed to obtain gauge.
Crochet hook H/8
Sewing needle
Optional: For comfort and warmth, a piece of polar fleece 16 (18 - 20)" / 40 (45 - 50) cm long × 4" / 10 cm wide for inside of hat

Sample in photograph knit in JCA / Reynolds Lopi #369 (MC) and #307 (A) and Berroco's Classic Mohair #B1212 (B) used double stranded

14 sts and 20 rows = 4" / 10 cm in St st using size 10 US (4 UK, 6 mm) needles.
Always check gauge to save time and to ensure correct yardage and correct fit!

HAT

With 2 dpns and A, cast on 4 sts. Work
I-cord as foll: K4, *do not turn work. Slide
sts to other end of needle to work next row
from RS and k4; rep from * for 1" / 2.5 cm.
Cut A. With MC, inc 1 st in each st on next
row—8 sts. Divide sts evenly over 4 dpns
(2 sts on each needle). Join and k all rnds,
inc 1 st at end of each needle every rnd
(therefore 4 sts increased every rnd) until
there are 52 (60 - 68) sts or 13 (15 - 17) sts
on each needle. K 4 (5 - 6) rnds even. With

B, k 4 rnds. Cut B. With MC, k 6 (7 - 8) rnds.
Divide for flaps: Sl 17 (19 - 21) sts to holder
for front flap, 9 (11 - 13) sts to holder for
left ear flap, 17 (19 - 21) sts to holder for
back flap, leave rem 9 (11 - 13) sts on
needle for right ear. Working back and forth
in garter st, dec 1 st each edge every other
row 3 (4 - 5) times as foll: K1, k2tog, k to
last 3 sts, k2tog, k1—3 sts rem. Bind off.
Sl sts for front flap to needle. Work in garter
st, dec 1 st each edge as for ear flap until
9 sts rem. Bind off. Repeat for right ear and
back flaps.

FINISHING

With MC and crochet hook, work row of sc
around all flaps. With B, make 2 very full
2" / 5 cm pom-poms and attach to earflaps.
Fold up front flap and sew in place. *Optional:*
Sew piece of polar fleece inside hat.

jumpsuit in angora with matching cap
• unisex • quickknit

A QuickKnit jumpsuit, in delicious angora, knit for the prince or princess in your life. Buttons adorn the left side shoulder as well as the leg openings, allowing for easy dressing and diaper changes. This jumpsuit is the ultimate luxury, both to knit and to wear.

To fit newborn (3 months - 6 months)
Finished chest: 19 (20 - 21)" / 48.5
(50.5 - 53.5) cm
Length, shoulder to hem: 16½
(17½ - 18½)" / 42 (44.5 - 47) cm
Head circumference: 15 (16 - 17)" / 37.5
(40 - 42.5) cm

Worsted weight yarn which will obtain gauge
given below
500 (565 - 630) yd. / 450 (510 - 567) m
Knitting needles, straight and 20" / 50 cm
circular needle, size 7 US (7 UK, 4.5 mm) or
size needed to obtain gauge
Double pointed needles (dpns), size 7 US
(7 UK, 4.5 mm)
Stitch holders and markers
Ten ½" / 1.5 cm buttons
*Sample in photograph knit in Lang/Berroco
Angora in #9936 Teal*

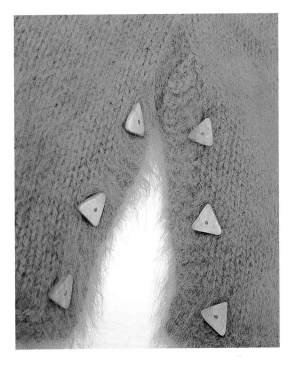

20 sts and 24 rows = 4" / 10 cm over St st
using size 7 US (7 UK, 4.5 mm) needles
*Always check gauge to save time and to ensure
correct yardage and correct fit!*

Cuff: Cast on 50 (52 - 54) sts. Work in garter st for 5 rows. *Next row (WS):* Work 4 sts in garter st, work in St st to last 4 sts, work last 4 sts in garter st. *Next row buttonhole, (RS):* K to last 5 sts, yo, k2tog, k3. Cont in pats as established, work buttonhole every 12 rows twice more and *at the same time,* inc 1 st each end every 4th row 5 times as foll: K4, inc, work to last 5 sts, inc in next st, k4. Work even on 60 (62 - 64) sts until piece measures 6½ (6¾ - 7)″ / 16.5 (17 - 17.5) cm from beg, end with a WS row. **Shape crotch:** Bind off 2 sts beg next 2 rows. Dec 1 st each

end every other row twice—52 (54 - 56) sts. Place sts on a holder.

Work same as left leg, working buttonholes at beg of RS rows as foll: K3, k2tog yo, work to end.

With RS of legs facing you, sl sts of right leg then left leg to circular needle, place marker for beg of rnd (center front). Work in rnds on 104 (108 - 112) sts in St st (k every rnd) until piece measures 8½ (9 - 9½)″ / 21.5 (23 - 24) cm from beg. *Next rnd:* K 24 (25 - 26), [k2tog] twice, k 48 (50 - 52), [k2tog] twice, k to end of rnd. Work 10 rnds even. *Next rnd:* K 23 (24 - 25), [k2tog] twice, k 46 (48 - 50), [k2tog] twice, k to end. Work even on 96 (100 - 104) sts until piece measures 11½ (12 - 12½)″ / 29 (30.5 - 31.5) cm from beg, cut yarn.

   Divide for armholes: Sl first 24 (25 - 26) sts and last 24 (25 - 26) sts to a holder for front. **Back:** Rejoin yarn and cont to work back and forth on 48 (50 - 52) back sts until piece measures 16½ (17½ - 18½)″ / 42 (44.5 - 47) cm from beg. *Next row (RS):* Work

13 (14 - 14) sts, sl these sts to holder for later finishing, bind off next 22 (22 - 24) sts for neck, work rem 13 (14 - 14) sts. Cont to work these sts in St st for 1" / 2.5 cm for button placket. Bind off.

Work as for back until piece measures 15 (16 - 17)" / 38 (40.5 - 43) cm from beg, end with a WS row.

Shape neck: *Next row (RS):* Work 19 (20 - 20) sts, join 2nd ball of yarn and bind off center 10 (10 - 12) sts, work to end. Working both sides at once, bind off from each neck edge 2 sts twice, 1 st twice, and *at the same time,* when piece measures 16 (17 - 18)" / 40.5 (43 - 45.5) cm from beg, work buttonholes on left front shoulder as foll: *Buttonhole row (RS):* [K2, yo, K2tog] 3 times, k rem sts. When piece measures

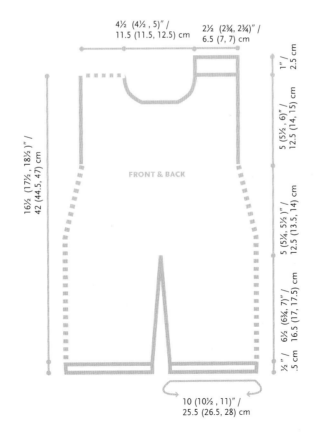

4½ (4½ , 5)" / 11.5 (11.5, 12.5) cm

2½ (2¾, 2¾)" / 6.5 (7, 7) cm

1" / 2.5 cm

5 (5½, 6)" / 12.5 (14, 15) cm

16½ (17½, 18½)" / 42 (44.5, 47) cm

FRONT & BACK

5 (5¼, 5½)" / 12.5 (13.5, 14) cm

6½ (6¾, 7)" / 16.5 (17, 17.5) cm

½" / .5 cm

10 (10½ , 11)" / 25.5 (26.5, 28) cm

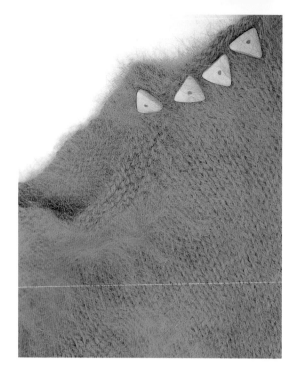

16½ (17½ - 18½)" / 42 (44.5 - 47) cm from beg, bind off left shoulder sts, place right shoulder sts on a holder for later finishing.

With *wrong sides facing* each other, and front of garment facing you, place sts of back and front right shoulders on two parallel dpns. With a third dpn, k first stitch from front needle tog with first stitch from back needle, *k next stitch from front and back needles tog, sl first st over 2nd st to bind off; rep from * until all sts are bound off. Cut yarn and pull end through last loop.

Sew buttons at left shoulder.

With dpns and RS facing, pick up and k 50 (52 - 55) sts around armhole (working through both layers on left side). Join, place marker for underarm seam. K 5 rnds, then dec 1 st each side of marker next rnd, then every 4th rnd 3 (3 - 2) times more, then every 2nd rnd 5 (6 - 8) times—32 (32 - 33) sts. Work even until sleeve measures 5 (5¼ - 5½)" / 12.5 (13.5 - 14) cm. [P 1 rnd, k1 rnd] twice, p1 rnd. Bind off loosely and evenly.

Sew front and back crotch seams. Sew buttons to legs.

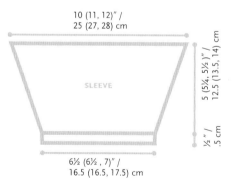

10 (11, 12)" / 25 (27, 28) cm

5 (5¼, 5½)" / 12.5 (13.5, 14) cm

SLEEVE

½" / .5 cm

6½ (6½ , 7)" / 16.5 (16.5, 17.5) cm

With RS facing, pick up and k 60 (60 - 64) sts evenly around neck edge. K 1 row. *Next row, buttonhole (RS):* K2, yo, k2tog, k to end. K 3 more rows. Bind off. Sew button to neckband.

HAT

With straight needles, cast on 75 (80 - 85) sts. Work in St st for 10 rows. *Next row (RS):* Cont in St st, inc 10 sts evenly across—85 (90 - 95) sts. Work even until piece measures 5½ (6 - 6½)" / 14 (15 - 16) cm from beg, end WS row. **Shape top:** Work dec rnds every other rnd 4 times as foll: *Dec rnd 1:* *K3, k2tog; rep from *—68 (72 - 76) sts. *Dec rnd 2:* *K2, k2tog; rep from *—51 (54 - 57) sts. *Dec rnd 3:* *K1, k2 tog; rep from *—34 (36 - 38) sts. *Dec rnd 4:* K2tog across—17 (18 - 19) sts. P2tog across next row, end p1 (0 - 1)—9 (9 - 10). K2tog across next row, end k 1 (1 - 0)—5 sts rem. Sl sts to dpns. Work I-cord as foll: *Do not turn work. Slide sts to other end of needle to work next row from RS and k5; rep from * for 3½" / 9 cm. Cut yarn and pull end through rem sts. Sew back seam, working seam on RS for first 10 rows of St st for rolled edge. Tie top knot.

Extraordinarily soft and warm, this nylon chenille jacket has an attached hood and toggle buttons. A true QuickKnit, perfect for newborns and babes-in-arms. I usually only use natural fibers, but this new yarn is like butter in your hands, and well worth trying.

To fit newborn (6 months - 12 months)
Finished chest (buttoned): 20 (21½ - 22¾)" / 50.5 (54.5 - 57.5) cm
Length, shoulder to hem: 9 (10 - 11)" / 23 (25.5 - 28) cm

Bulky weight wool which will obtain gauge given below
200 (250 - 300) yd. / 185 (230 - 275) m
Knitting needles, size 9 US (5 UK, 5.5 mm) or size needed to obtain gauge
Double pointed needles (dpns), size 9 US (5 UK, 5.5 mm)
Stitch holders and markers
Three ¾" / 2 cm buttons
Sample in photograph knit in Berroco Plush in #1905 Powder Pink

12 sts and 16 rows = 4" / 10 cm over St st using size 9 US (5 UK, 5.5 mm) needles
Always check gauge to save time and to ensure correct yardage and correct fit!

Cast on 30 (32 - 34) sts. K 2 rows. Work in St st until piece measures 9 (10 - 11)" / 23 (25.5 - 28) cm from beg, end with a WS row. K 8 (9 - 9) sts and place on a holder for right shoulder, k next 14 (14 -16) sts and place on a 2nd holder for back neck, k rem sts and place on a 3rd holder for left shoulder.

Cast on 17 (18 - 19) sts. K 2 rows. *Next row (RS):* Work 14 (15 - 16) sts in St st, work last 3 sts in garter st for buttonband. Cont as

established until piece measures 7½ (8½ - 9½)" / 19 (21.5 - 24) cm from beg, end with a WS row. **Shape neck:** *Next row (RS):* Work to last 3 sts, place 3 sts on a holder. *Next row:* Bind off 3 (3 - 4) sts (neck edge), work to end. Cont to bind off from neck edge 3 sts once more—8 (9 - 9) sts. Work even until piece measures same length as back. Place rem 8 (9 - 9) sts on a holder for later finishing. Place markers on band for 3 buttons, the first ½" / 1.5 cm below neck edge and two other spaced 2" / 5 cm apart.

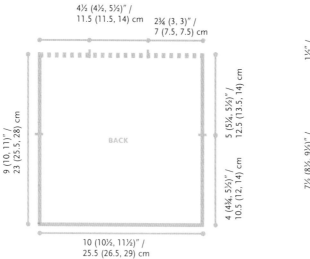

4½ (4½, 5½)" / 11.5 (11.5, 14) cm
2¾ (3, 3)" / 7 (7.5, 7.5) cm

9 (10, 11)" / 23 (25.5, 28) cm

BACK

5 (5¼, 5½)" / 12.5 (13.5, 14) cm

4 (4¾, 5½)" / 10.5 (12, 14) cm

10 (10½, 11½)" / 25.5 (26.5, 29) cm

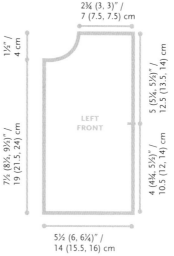

2¾ (3, 3)" / 7 (7.5, 7.5) cm

1½" / 4 cm

LEFT FRONT

7½ (8½, 9½)" / 19 (21.5, 24) cm

5 (5¼, 5½)" / 12.5 (13.5, 14) cm

4 (4¾, 5½)" / 10.5 (12, 14) cm

5½ (6, 6¼)" / 14 (15.5, 16) cm

Cast on 17 (18 - 19) sts. K 2 rows. *Next row (RS):* Work 3 sts in garter st for buttonhole band, work 14 (15 - 16) sts in St st. Cont to work sts as established, reversing neck shaping, and working buttonholes opposite markers as foll: *Buttonhole row (RS):* K3, yo, k2tog, k to end.

With *wrong sides facing* each other, and front of sweater facing you, place sts of back and front right shoulders on two parallel dpns. With a third dpn, k first stitch from front needle tog with first stitch from back needle, *k next stitch from front and back needles

tog, sl first st over 2nd st to bind off; rep from * until all sts are bound off. Cut yarn and pull end through last loop.

Mark for sleeves 5 (5¼ - 5½)" / 12.5 (13.5 - 14) cm down from shoulder seam on front and back. With RS facing, pick up and k 30 (32 - 34) sts between markers. Work in St st for 5 rows, then dec 1 st each end on next row, then every 4th row 2 (4 - 4) times, every 2nd row 2 (0 - 1) times—20 (22 - 22) sts. Work even until sleeve measures 5 (6 - 6½)" / 12.5 (15.5 - 16.5) cm, end with a RS row. K 2 rows, then bind off loosely and evenly.

With RS facing, pick up and k 8 (9 - 9) sts between holder and shoulder seam, place marker, k 7 (7 - 8) sts from back neck holder, place marker, k rem sts from back neck holder, place marker, pick up and k 8 (9 - 9) sts along left front neck—30 (32 - 34) sts. Work in St st for 3 rows. Next (inc) row: K, inc 1 st before and after each marker—6 sts

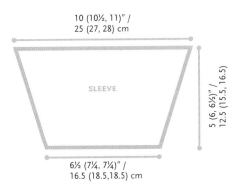

10 (10½, 11)" /
25 (27, 28) cm

SLEEVE

5 (6, 6½)" /
12.5 (15.5, 16.5)

6½ (7¼, 7¼)" /
16.5 (18.5, 18.5) cm

increased. Work 1 row even. Rep last 2 rows twice more —48 (50 - 52) sts. Work even until hood measures 7½ (8 - 8)" / 19 (20.5 - 20.5) cm. Fold hood in half and divide sts evenly over 2 dpn. K sts tog same as shoulder seams. *Hood edging:* Sl 3 sts of left front holder onto needle and cont in garter st until piece fits along outside edge of hood. Sew edge of band along hood, adjusting length if necessary. Weave rem 3 sts tog with sts on right front holder.

FINISHING

Sew side and sleeve seams. Sew on buttons.

To fit newborn to 6 months (12 months -
18 months)
Finished head circircumference: 16 (18 - 20)" /
40 (45 - 50) cm

Worsted weight wool that will obtain gauge
given below
100 (115 - 130 -150) yd. / 90 (105 - 120 - 140)
m (MC), 50 (60 - 70 - 80) yd. / 45
(55 - 65 - 75) m (CC)
Knitting needles, straight size 8 US (6 UK,
5 mm) or size needed to obtain gauge
Small piece of cardboard for snowballs
Sewing needle
Optional: For comfort and warmth, a piece of
polar fleece 16 (18 - 20)" / 40 (45 - 50) cm
long × 4" / 10 cm wide for inside of hat

*Sample in photograph knit in Brown Sheep
Lamb's Pride Black (MC) and White (CC)*

18 sts and 20 rows = 4" / 10 cm in St st
using size 8 US (6 UK, 5 mm) needles.
*Always check gauge to save time and to
ensure correct yardage and correct fit!*

Rows 1, 3, 5, 7, and 9 (WS): With MC, p.

Rows 2, 4, 6, 8, and 10: With MC, k.

Rows 11 and 13: P 0 (1 - 0) st CC, *p 1 st MC, p 1 st CC; rep from *.

Rows 12 and 14: K 1 st MC, k 1 st CC; rep from *, end K 0 (1 - 0) MC.

Cast on 62 (71 - 80) sts. Work rows 1–10 of stripe pat, inc 10 sts evenly across last row—72 (81 - 90) sts. Cont in stripe pat until piece measures 6½" / 16 cm from cast on edge, end WS row. *Next row, dec row 1 (RS):* *K7, k2tog; rep from *—64 (72 - 80) sts. Cont in stripe pat and *at the same time* work dec row [every 8th row, then every 4th row] 3 times, then every 8th row once more as foll:

Dec row 2: *K6, k2tog; rep from *—56 (63 - 70) sts rem.

Dec row 3: *K5, k2tog; rep from *—48 (54 - 60) sts rem.

Dec row 4: *K4, k2tog; rep from *—40 (45 - 50) sts rem.

Dec row 5: *K3, k2tog; rep from *—32 (36 - 40) sts rem.

Dec row 6: *K2, k2tog; rep from *—24 (27 - 30) sts rem.

Dec row 7: *K1, k2tog; rep from *—16 (18 - 20) sts rem.

Work 2 more rows. K2tog across—8 (9 - 10) sts. Cut yarn leaving long end. Pull yarn through rem sts and sew back seam, working seam on RS for last 2" / 5 cm so that it's invisible when bottom edge rolls up.

With CC, wind yarn around 2" / 5 cm wide piece of cardboard about 13 times. Cut yarn. Remove from cardboard. Cut 6" / 15 cm piece and tie tightly around middle. Cut loops and trim. Sew to top of hat. Sew 1 snowball to each solid color stripe, staggering them around hat. *Optional:* Sew piece of polar fleece to inside of hat.

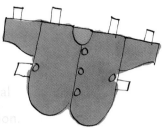

With unusual rounded bottom shaping and sides that are buttoned rather than seamed, this cardigan trimmed with many buttons has real flair. The perfect garment for using various buttons from your collection.

To fit newborn to 3 months (6–12 months - 18–24 months)
Finished chest (buttoned): 19 (22 - 25)" / 48 (56 - 63.5) cm
Length, shoulder to hem: 9 (11 - 13)" / 23 (28 - 33) cm

Bulky weight yarn which will obtain gauge given below.
160 (220 - 290) yd. / 145 (200 - 260) m
Knitting needles sizes 7 and 9 US (7 and 5 UK, 4.5 and 5.5 mm) or size needed to obtain gauge
Double pointed needles (dpns), size 7 US (7 UK, 4.5 mm)
Stitch holders and markers
Five assorted 1" / 2.5 cm buttons
Sample in photograph knit in Berroco Chinchilla in #5422 Purple

14 sts and 20 rows = 4" / 10 cm over St st using size 7 US (7 UK, 4.5 mm) needles
Always check gauge to save time and to ensure correct yardage and correct fit!

First scallop: With larger needle, cast on 18 (20 - 23) sts. K 1 row. Change to smaller needles. Work in short rows as foll: *Row 1 (RS):* K 10 (11 - 13), sl 1, turn. *Row 2 (WS):* P 5 (6 - 7), sl 1, turn. *Row 3:* K 7 (8 - 10), sl 1, turn. *Row 4:* P 9 (10 - 12), sl 1, turn. *Row 5:* K 11 (12 - 13), sl, 1, turn. *Row 6:* P 12 (14 - 15), sl 1, turn. *Row 7:* K 13 (16 - 17), sl 1, turn. *Row 8:* P 14 (17 - 18), sl 1, turn. *Row 9:* K 15 (18 - 19), sl 1, turn. *For size 18–24 months only:* Row 10: P20, sl 1. Row 11: K22, sl 1. Row 12: P. Row 13: K. *For other sizes:* Row 10: P. Row 11: K. Place 18 (20 - 23) sts on a holder.

Second scallop: Work same as first scallop, then work sts from holder. Cont in St st over all 36 (40 - 46) sts until piece measures 9 (11 - 13)" / 23 (28 - 33) cm from beg (measured from beg of scallop), end with a WS row. Work 11 (12 - 14) sts and place on a holder for right shoulder, bind off next 14 (16 - 18) sts for back neck, work rem sts and place on a 2nd holder for left shoulder.

Work same as first scallop of back, then cont in St st until piece measures 7½ (9½ - 11)" / 19 (24 - 28) cm from beg (measured from beg of scallop), end with a RS row. **Shape neck:** *Next row (WS):* Bind off 4 sts (neck edge), work to end. Cont to bind off from neck edge 2 sts 1 (2 - 2) times, 1 st 1 (0 - 1) times. When same length as back, place rem 11 (12 - 14) sts on a holder for later finishing. Place markers on front edge for 3 buttons, the first one just above scallop, the last one ½" / 1.5 cm below neck shaping, and the third one in between.

Work to correspond to left front, reversing neck shaping and working buttonholes opposite markers as foll: *Buttonhole row (RS):* K2, bind off 2, k to end. *Next row:* Cast on 2 sts over bound off sts.

With *wrong sides facing* each other, and front of sweater facing you, place sts of back and front right shoulders on two parallel dpns. With a third dpn, k first stitch from front needle tog with first stitch from back needle, *k next stitch from front and back needles tog, sl first st over 2nd st to bind off; rep from * until all sts are bound off. Cut yarn and pull end through last loop.

SLEEVES

Mark for sleeves 5 (5½ - 6)″ / 12.5 (14 - 15.5) cm down from shoulder seam on front and back. With RS facing, pick up and k 36 (38 - 42) sts between markers. Work in St st

for 5 rows, then dec 1 st each end on next row, then every 4th row 2 (4 - 5) times, every 2nd row 4 (3 - 3) times more—22 (22 - 24) sts. Work even until sleeve measures 5 (6 - 7)″ / 12.5 (15.5 - 17.5) cm, end with a RS row. K 2 rows, then bind off loosely and evenly.

FINISHING

Sew sleeve seams. At side edges, overlap front over back and sew a button 6¼″ (8¼ - 10)″ / 16 (21 - 25.5) cm down from shoulder. Sew buttons to left front.

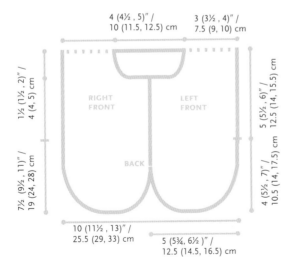

4 (4½ , 5)″ /
10 (11.5, 12.5) cm

3 (3½ , 4)″ /
7.5 (9, 10) cm

1½ (1½ , 2)″ /
4 (4, 5) cm

RIGHT
FRONT

LEFT
FRONT

BACK

7½ (9½ , 11)″ /
19 (24, 28) cm

5 (5½ , 6)″ /
12.5 (14, 15.5) cm

4 (5½ , 7)″ /
10.5 (14, 17.5) cm

10 (11½ , 13)″ /
25.5 (29, 33) cm

5 (5¾, 6½)″ /
12.5 (14.5, 16.5) cm

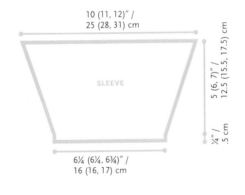

10 (11, 12)″ /
25 (28, 31) cm

SLEEVE

5 (6, 7)″ /
12.5 (15.5, 17.5) cm

¼″ /
.5 cm

6¼ (6¼, 6¾)″ /
16 (16, 17) cm

zing!

zany, colorful delights

Babies are darling in pure, clear colors, and

we are all entranced with piquant color

combinations on a baby. Try frosty pink with

orange, saucy green with icy aqua, and give

the traditional a twist.

vestimenti
bulky vest with soutache trim
• *unisex* • *quickknit*

Knit in a snap, this vest has a playful array of spirals. Create your own colorways, or even write a child's name; this is the perfect opportunity to spread your creative wings.

SIZES

To fit newborn (6 months - 1 year - 2 years)
Finished chest (buttoned): 19 (21 - 24 - 26)" / 48.5 (53.5 - 61 - 66) cm
Length, shoulder to hem: 9 (10 - 12 - 13)" / 23 (25.5 - 30.5 - 33) cm

MATERIALS

Bulky weight yarn which will obtain gauge given below
110 (140 - 180 - 220) yd. / 100
(126 - 162 - 200) m (MC)
Small amounts of two contrasting colors (A) and (B)
Knitting needles, size 10 US (4 UK, 6 mm) or size needed to obtain gauge
Double pointed needles (dpns), size 10 US (4 UK, 6 mm)
Crochet hook, size H/8 for chain swirls
Stitch holders and markers
Four (4 - 5 - 5) 1" / 2.5 cm buttons

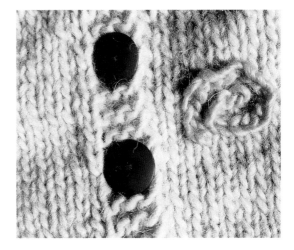

Sample in photograph knit in JCA/Reynolds Lopi in #369 Light Green (MC), #113 Light Blue (A), and #0212 Dark Green (B)

GAUGE

14 sts and 20 rows = 4" / 10 cm over St st using size 10 US (4 UK, 6 mm) needles
Always check gauge to save time and to ensure correct yardage and correct fit!

BODY

With MC, cast on 70 (77 - 88 - 94) sts. Work in garter st for 4 rows. *Next row (RS):* Work 3 sts in garter st, work in St st to last 3 sts, work 3 sts in garter st. Cont in pat as established. *Buttonhole row (RS):* K1, k2tog, yo, work to end. Rep buttonhole row every 2 (2½ - 2¼ - 2½)″ / 5 (6.5 - 6 - 6.5) cm 3 (3 - 4 - 4) times more, and *at the same time,* when piece measures 5 (5½ - 7 - 7½)″ / 12.5 (14 - 17.5 - 19) cm from beg, end with a WS row and work as foll:

DIVIDE FOR FRONT AND BACK

Next row (RS): Work 13 (15 - 17 - 18) sts and place on a holder for right front, bind off next 10 (10 - 12 - 12) sts for armhole, work until there are 24 (27 - 30 - 34) sts for back.

Place rem 23 (25 - 29 - 30) sts on a holder for left front. Cont on back sts only, working first and last 3 sts in garter st for armhole edging, until piece measures 9 (10 - 12 - 13)″ / 23 (25.5 - 30.5 - 33) cm from beg, end WS row. Work 5 (6 - 6 - 8) sts and place on a holder for right shoulder, bind off next 14 (15 - 18 - 18) sts for neck, work rem sts and place on a 2nd holder for left shoulder.

LEFT FRONT

Next row (RS): Slip 23 (25 - 29 - 30) sts from left front holder to needle. Rejoin yarn at armhole edge and bind off 10 (10 - 12 - 12) sts for armhole, work to end. Cont on rem 13 (15 - 17 - 18) sts, working first and last 3 sts in garter st, until piece measures 7½ (8½ - 10 - 11)″ / 19 (21.5 - 25.5 - 28) cm from beg, end with a WS row. **Shape neck:** *Next row (RS):* Work to last 3 sts, place 3 sts on a holder. *Next row:* Bind off 2 (3 - 3 - 3) sts (neck edge), work to end. Cont to bind off from neck edge 2 (2 - 3 - 2) sts once, then 1 (1 - 2 - 2) sts once. When same length as back, place rem 5 (6 - 6 - 8) sts on a holder for later finishing.

RIGHT FRONT

Work to correspond to left front, cont to work buttonholes as established and reverse neck shaping.

SHOULDER SEAMS

With *wrong sides facing* each other, and front of sweater facing you, place sts of back and front right shoulders on two parallel dpns. With a third dpn, k first stitch from front needle tog with first stitch from back needle, *k next stitch from front and back needles tog, sl first st over 2nd st to bind off; rep from * until all sts are bound off. Cut yarn and pull end through last loop.

FINISHING

Neckband

With RS facing and MC, k 3 sts from right front holder, pick up and k 32 (34 - 40 - 40) sts around neck, k 3 sts from left front holder—38 (40 - 46 - 46) sts. K 3 rows. Bind off.

Chain Swirls

With crochet hook and A or B, chain 18. Fasten off. Curl chains to form swirls and sew to body as desired. Sew on buttons.

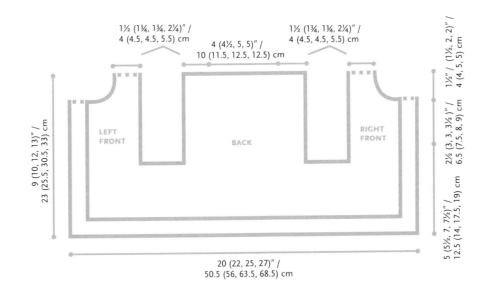

1½ (1¾, 1¾, 2¼)" / 4 (4.5, 4.5, 5.5) cm

4 (4½, 5, 5)" / 10 (11.5, 12.5, 12.5) cm

1½ (1¾, 1¾, 2¼)" / 4 (4.5, 4.5, 5.5) cm

1½" / (1¾, 2, 2)" / 4 (4, 5, 5) cm

2¼ (3, 3, 3½)" / 6.5 (7.5, 8, 9) cm

9 (10, 12, 13)" / 23 (25.5, 30.5, 33) cm

LEFT FRONT

BACK

RIGHT FRONT

5 (5½, 7, 7½)" / 12.5 (14, 17.5, 19) cm

20 (22, 25, 27)" / 50.5 (56, 63.5, 68.5) cm

gelati

pullover with purl stitch lattice pattern

• worsted weight yarn • unisex

The simple lattice pattern in this pullover is quite easy once you get the pattern going. Done in a luxurious cashmere, this is a sweater for parties and holidays. Or try it in worsted cotton for a summer charmer.

SIZES

To fit: 3 to 6 months (18–24 months - 3 years)
Finished chest: 19 (24½ - 30)" / 48 (62 - 76) cm
Length, shoulder to hem: 9½ (11½ - 14)" / 24 (29 - 35.5) cm

MATERIALS

Heavy worsted weight yarn which will obtain gauge given below
210 (320 - 420) yd. / 190 (288 - 378) m
Knitting needles, sizes 9 and 10 US (5 and 4 UK, 5.5 and 6 mm) or size needed to obtain gauge
16" / 40 cm circular needle, size 9 US (5 UK, 5.5 mm)
Double pointed needles (dpns), size 9 US (5 UK, 5.5 mm)
Stitch holders and markers
Sample in photograph knit in Trendsetter Dahli #187 Red

GAUGE

14 sts and 22 rows = 4" / 10 cm over chart pat using size 10 US (4 UK, 6 mm) needles
Always check gauge to save time and to ensure correct yardage and correct fit!

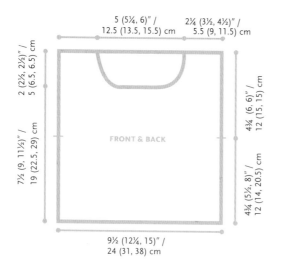

row: Work 8 (12 - 16) sts and place on a holder for right shoulder, bind off next 17 (19 - 21) sts for back neck, k rem sts and place on a 2nd holder for left shoulder.

FRONT

Work as for back until piece measures 7½ (9 - 11½)" / 19 (22.5 - 29) cm from beg, end WS row. **Shape neck:** Work 13 (17 - 21) sts, join 2nd ball of yarn and bind off center 7 (9 - 11) sts, work to end. Working both sides at same time, bind off from each neck edge 2 sts once, 1 st 3 times. Work even until same length as back. Place rem 8 (12 - 16) sts each side on holders for later finishing.

BACK

With smaller needles, cast on 33 (43 - 53) sts. Work in k1, p1 rib for 2 rows. Change to larger needles and work in chart pat as foll: K1, work 10-st rep of chart 3 (4 - 5) times, work first st of rep once more, k1. Cont in pat as established until 50 (60 - 75) rows have been worked in chart pat. Piece measures approx 9½ (11½ - 14)" / 24 (29 - 35.5) cm from beg, end WS row. *Next*

5 (5¼, 6)" / 12.5 (13.5, 15.5) cm

2¼ (3½, 4½)" / 5.5 (9, 11.5) cm

2 (2½, 2½)" / 5 (6.5, 6.5) cm

4¾ (6, 6)" / 12 (15, 15) cm

7½ (9, 11½)" / 19 (22.5, 29) cm

FRONT & BACK

4¾ (5½, 8)" / 12 (14, 20.5) cm

9½ (12¼, 15)" / 24 (31, 38) cm

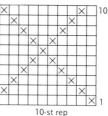

Stitch key

☐ St st

☒ Rev St st

10

1

10-st rep

SHOULDER SEAMS

With *wrong sides facing* each other, and front of sweater facing you, place sts of back and front right shoulders on two parallel dpns. With a third dpn, k first stitch from front needle tog with first stitch from back needle, *k next stitch from front and back needles tog, sl first st over 2nd st to bind off; rep from * until all sts are bound off. Cut yarn and pull end through last loop.

SLEEVES

Mark for sleeves 4¾ (6 - 6)" / 12 (15 - 15) cm down from shoulder seam on front and back. With RS facing, pick up and k 33 (43 - 43) sts between markers. Work in chart pat same as back, *at the same time*, work 5 rows

even, then dec 1 st each end (working dec sts into chart pat) on next row, then every 6th (4th - 4th) row 3 (6 - 7) times, every 4th (2nd - 2nd) row 1 (2 - 1) times—23 (25 - 25) sts. Work even until sleeve measures 5½ (6½ - 7)" / 14 (16.5 - 17.5) cm, end with a WS row. Change to smaller needles and work in k1, p1 rib for 2 rows. Bind off loosely and evenly in rib.

FINISHING

Sew side and sleeve seams.

Neckband

With RS facing and circular needle, pick up and k 54 (58 - 62) sts evenly around neck edge. Join and work in k1, p1 rib for 2 rows. Bind off in rib.

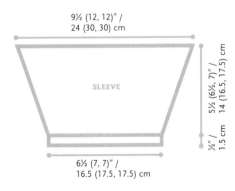

9½ (12, 12)" /
24 (30, 30) cm

SLEEVE

5½ (6½, 7)" / 14 (16.5, 17.5) cm

½" / 1.5 cm

6½ (7, 7)" /
16.5 (17.5, 17.5) cm

feltie chapeau

felted madeleine hat • felted bulky wool
• unisex • quickknit

This felted hat with a rolled brim has been knit in Brown Sheep Bulky Wool. Although yardage is given, because this is felted, I recommend trying to get this wonderful wool. After felting, simply cut small slits in the fabric and pull ribbons through. Color choices and ribbons make this appropriate for either boys or girls.

SIZES

6 months (12 months - 18 – 24 months)
Circumference (after felting): 16 (18 - 20)" / 40.5 (45.5 - 50.5) cm
Note: The finished size of a felted hat can be affected by the type of yarn you are using as well as the temperature of water in your washing machine. The measurements here are consequently approximate, and it may take some experimentation to achieve the desired size. Adding or subtracting 5 sts to the cast-on sts will adjust the circumference by approx 2" / 5 cm.

MATERIALS

Following are approx amts based on using Brown Sheep Lamb's Pride Bulky yarn (M180, Ruby Red). Other yarns and colors may felt more or less making a smaller or larger garment and thus may require different amounts of yarn to achieve the desired size.

85 (110 - 205) yd. / 77 (100 - 185) m
16" / 40 cm circular needle and dpns, size 10.5 US (3 UK, 6.5 mm)
48" / 120 cm, ¾"- / 2 cm ribbon

GAUGE

12 sts = 4" / 10 cm over St st using size 10.5 US (3 UK, 6.5 mm) needles (before felting)
Always check gauge to save time and to ensure correct yardage and correct fit!

HAT

With circular needle, cast on 65 (75 - 85) sts.
Join, taking care not to twist sts.

Rnds 1–10: Knit.

Rnd 11: *K 4 (5 - 6), k2tog; rep from * 9
times more, end k5—55 (65 - 75) sts.

Rnds 12–16: Knit.

Rnd 17: *K 3 (4 - 5), k2tog; rep from * 9
times more, end k5—45 (55 - 65) sts.

Rnds 18–32: Knit.

Change to dpns for crown.

Rnd 33: *K 5, k2tog; rep from *, end k 3
(6 - 2) sts—39 (48 - 56) sts.

Rnds 34, 36, and 38: Knit.

Rnd 35: *K4, k2tog; rep from *, end
k 3 (0 - 2) sts—33 (40 - 47) sts.

Rnd 37: *K3, k2tog; rep from *, end
k 3 (0 - 2) sts—27 (32 - 38) sts.

Rnd 39: *K2, k2tog; rep from *, end
k 3 (0 - 2) sts—21 (24 - 29) sts.

Rnd 40: *K2tog; rep from * to last 3 (0 - 3)
sts, end k3tog (0 - k3tog)—10 (12 - 14) sts.
Divide rem sts onto two needles and weave
sts tog. Weave in all ends.

FELTING

Note: Due to temperature fluctuations,
felting time will vary. Check often for
sizing.

In washing machine, set on hot wash/
cold rinse for a small load, place hat in
water and run through longest cycle.
Check, then run through again. Remove
and shape hat over round-bottomed bowl
approx the size of head. Roll brim and let
dry. Cut small slits at each side of hat near
brim. Cut 2 pieces of 18" / 45 cm ribbon
and tie single knot at one end of each
piece; thread through.

english trifle

pullover with duplicate stitch and ruffles
• unisex • sport weight wool

Perfect for holidays and parties, this pullover has a ruffled neckline, reverse stockinette striped ridges and duplicate stitch bird's-eye embroidery. Darling and piquant, a delectable delight in wool.

SIZES

To fit 3 to 6 months (1 year - 2 years - 3 years)
Finished chest: 19 (23 - 25 - 27)" / 48.5
(58.5 - 63.5 - 68.5) cm
Length, shoulder to hem: 9 (11 - 12 - 13)" /
22.5 (28 - 31 - 33) cm

MATERIALS

Worsted weight yarn which will obtain gauge
given below
245 (350 - 420 - 490) yd. /
225 (315 - 380 - 440) m (MC)
60 (85 - 100 - 120) yd. /
54 (77 - 90 - 108) m (A)
10 (15 - 20) yd. / 9 (14 - 18) m (B)
Knitting needles, straight and 16" circular,
size 7 US (7 UK, 4.5 mm) or size needed to
obtain gauge
Double pointed needles (dpns), size 7 US
(7 UK, 4.5 mm)
Stitch holders and markers
Yarn needle

Sample in photograph knit in Brown Sheep Naturespun #245 Pink Diamond (MC), #N54 Orange (A) and #861 Dark Orange (B)

GAUGE

20 sts and 35 rows = 4" / 10 cm over stripe
pat using size 7 US (7 UK, 4.5 mm) needles
*Always check gauge to save time and to ensure
correct yardage and correct fit!*

STRIPE PATTERN

Rows 1–8: With MC, beg with a knit row, work in St st.

Row 9 (RS): With A, knit.

Rows 10 and 12: With A, knit.

Row 11: With A, purl.

Rep rows 1–12 for stripe pat.

BACK

With straight needles and MC, cast on 48 (58 - 62 - 68) sts. Work in k1, p1 rib for ½" / 1.5 cm, end WS row. Work 6 (7 - 8 - 9) repeats of stripe pat, then work next 4 (8 - 4 - 2) rows; piece measures approx 9 (11 - 12 - 13)" / 22.5 (28 - 31 - 33) cm from beg. K 13 (17 - 19 - 20) and place on a holder for right shoulder, bind off next 22 (24 - 24 - 28) sts for back neck, k rem sts and place on a 2nd holder for left shoulder.

FRONT

Work same as back until piece measures 7½ (9½ - 10½ - 11½)" / 18.5 (24 - 27 - 29) cm from beg, end WS. **Shape neck:** *Next row (RS):* Work 18 (22 - 24 - 26) sts, join 2nd ball of yarn and bind off center 12 (14 - 14 - 16) sts, work to end. Working both sides at same time, bind off from each neck edge 2 (2 - 2 - 3) sts once, then dec 1 st every other row 3 times. Work even until same length as back. Place rem 13 (17 - 19 - 20) sts for each side on holders for later finishing.

SHOULDER SEAMS

With *wrong sides facing* each other, and front of sweater facing you, place sts of back and front right shoulders on two parallel dpns. With a third dpn, k first stitch from front needle tog with first stitch from back needle, *k next stitch from front and back needles tog, sl first st over 2nd st to bind off; rep from * until all sts are bound off. Cut yarn and pull end through last loop.

SLEEVES

Mark for sleeves 5 (5½ - 6 - 6½)" / 12.5 (14 - 15.5 - 16.5) cm down from shoulder seam on front and back. With RS facing, pick up and k 50 (56 - 60 - 66) sts between markers. Cont in stripe pat, and *at the same time*, work 5 rows even after pick-up row, then dec 1 st each end on next row, then every 6th row 2 (3 - 2 - 1) times, every 4th row 6 (7 - 10 - 13) times—32 (34 - 34 - 36) sts. Work even until sleeve measures 5 (6¼ - 6¾ - 7½)" / 12.5 (16 - 17 - 19) cm. With MC, work in k1, p1 rib for ½" / 1.5 cm. Bind off loosely and evenly in rib.

Bird's-eye embroidery: With B, embroider bird's-eye pat using duplicate st on every other MC stripe as foll: On 6th row, embroider 3rd st, on 3rd row, embroider the 6th st. Cont to embroider every 6th st, alternating between 6th row and 3rd row.

FINISHING

Sew side and sleeve seams.

Neckband

With RS facing, MC and circular needle or dpns, pick up and k 64 (68 - 68 - 76) sts evenly around neck edge. Join and work in k3, p1 rib for 4 rnds. Work next rnd as foll: K in front and back of each st—128 (136 - 136 - 152) sts. Work in k4, p4 rib for 1" / 2.5 cm. Bind off in rib.

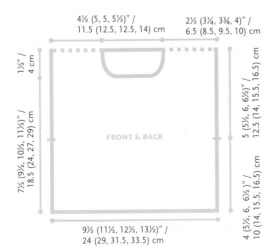

4½ (5, 5, 5½)" / 11.5 (12.5, 12.5, 14) cm

2½ (3¼, 3¾, 4)" / 6.5 (8.5, 9.5, 10) cm

1½" / 4 cm

7½ (9½, 10½, 11½)" / 18.5 (24, 27, 29) cm

FRONT & BACK

5 (5½, 6, 6½)" / 12.5 (14, 15.5, 16.5) cm

4 (5½, 6, 6½)" / 10 (14, 15.5, 16.5) cm

9½ (11½, 12½, 13½)" / 24 (29, 31.5, 33.5) cm

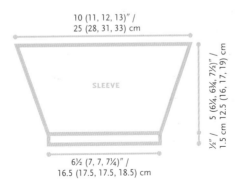

10 (11, 12, 13)" / 25 (28, 31, 33) cm

SLEEVE

5 (6¼, 6¾, 7½)" / 12.5 (16, 17, 19) cm

½" / 1.5 cm

6½ (7, 7, 7¼)" / 16.5 (17.5, 17.5, 18.5) cm

mini pini

jumper or sundress in soft cotton with shoulder buttons
• girls • quickknit

Working either as a sundress or jumper, this dress has a simple garter stitch bottom border. Very easily knit, this is a charmer. Make sure you get your correct gauge when working with cotton, especially for the ribbed bodice. I generally go down at least one needle size when working with cotton; crisp fabric is the ideal here.

SIZES

To fit 3 to 6 months (12 months - 18 months)
Finished chest: 14 (17 - 19)" / 35.5 (43 - 48.5) cm
Length, shoulder to hem: 11½ (14½ - 15)" / 29 (37 - 38) cm

MATERIALS

DK weight yarn which will obtain gauge given below
310 (465 - 550) yd. / 280 (420 - 495) m
Knitting needles, straight size 5 US (3.75 mm) or size needed to obtain gauge
Circular needles, size 5 US (8 UK, 4 mm) 16" / 40 cm and 29" / 72 cm long.
Two 1" / 2.5 cm buttons
Sample in photograph knit in Reynolds/JCA Saucy Sport in #143 Yellow

GAUGE

22 sts and 28 rows = 4" / 10 cm over St st using size 5 US (3.75 mm) needles
Always check gauge to save time and to ensure correct yardage and correct fit!

SKIRT

With longer circular needle, cast on 176 (208 - 240) sts. Join, taking care not to twist sts on needle. Place marker for beg of rnd. Work in garter st (k 1 rnd, p 1 rnd) for 14 rnds. Cont in St st (k every rnd) until piece measures 6½ (8 - 8¼)" / 16.5 (20.5 - 21) cm from beg. *Next row:* K2tog around—88 (104 - 120) sts. Change to shorter circular needle if necessary.

BODICE

Work in k1, p1 rib for 2 rnds. Divide for front and back: Work 44 (52 - 60) sts for front, place rem sts on a holder for back.

FRONT

Shape armhole: Working back and forth in rib, bind off 2 sts at beg of next 2 rows, dec 1 st each end every other row 3 (3 - 4) times—34 (42 - 48) sts. Work even until

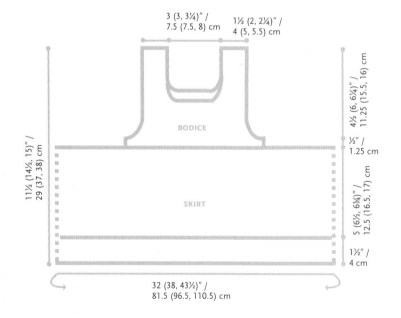

3 (3, 3¼)" /
7.5 (7.5, 8) cm

1½ (2, 2¼)" /
4 (5, 5.5) cm

BODICE

SKIRT

11½ (14½, 15)" /
29 (37, 38) cm

4½ (6, 6¼)" /
11.25 (15.5, 16) cm

½" /
1.25 cm

5 (6½, 6¾)" /
12.5 (16.5, 17) cm

1½" /
4 cm

32 (38, 43½)" /
81.5 (96.5, 110.5) cm

bodice measures 1½ (2¼ - 2½)" / 4 (6 - 6.5) cm, end with a WS row. **Shape neck:** Work 12 (16 - 18) sts, join 2nd skein of yarn and bind off center 10 (10 - 12) sts, work to end. Working both sides at same time, dec 1 st at each neck edge every other row 3 (5 - 5) times—9 (11 - 13) sts. Work even in rib until bodice measures 4 (5½ - 5¾)" / 10 (14 - 14.5) cm. *Next row, buttonhole:* For each side, rib 3 (4 - 5), yo, k2tog, rib to end. Rib 3 rows more. Bind off sts each side in rib.

Work as for front, but work neck shaping when bodice measures 2 (3½ - 3¾)" / 5 (9 - 9.5) cm, as foll: **Shape neck:** Work 12 (16 - 18) sts, join 2nd skein of yarn and bind off center 10 (10 - 12) sts, work to end. Working both sides at once, dec 1 st at each neck edge every other row 3 (5 - 5) times—9 (11 - 13) sts. Work even, omitting buttonholes, until same length as front. Bind off sts each side in rib.

FINISHING

Sew buttons on shoulders.

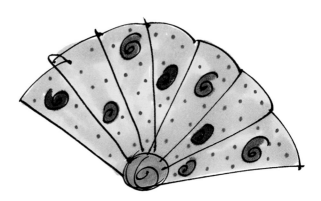

colori

striped pullover with shoulder buttons

• cotton chenille • unisex • quickknit

Bright, icy pastels make this QuickKnit pullover an out-of-the-ordinary project. Take care to pull your stitches tightly to achieve a firm, even fabric. This soft cotton chenille is perfect for babies and toddlers for everyday wear.

SIZES

3 to 6 months (1 year - 2 years - 3 years)
Finished chest: 20 (23 - 25 - 27)" / 51
(58.5 - 63.5 - 68.5) cm
Length, shoulder to hem: 10 (12 - 13 - 14)" /
25 (30.5 - 33 - 35.5) cm

MATERIALS

Heavy worsted weight yarn that will obtain
gauge given below
200 (280 - 330 - 380) yd. / 180
(252 - 297 - 342) m (MC)
60 (80 - 90 - 110) yd. / 54 (72 - 81 - 100)
m (CC)
Knitting needles, 20" / 50 cm or longer
Circular needle, size 9 US (5 UK, 5.5 mm) or
size needed to obtain gauge
Double pointed needles (dpns), size 9 US
(5 UK, 5.5 mm)
Stitch holders and markers
Three ½" / 1.5 cm buttons

Sample in photograph knit in Crystal Palace
Chenille #1802 Blue (MC) and #2342 Green
(CC) with needles size 5 US (9 UK, 3.75 mm)

GAUGE

16 sts and 28 rows = 4" / 10 cm in St st
Always check gauge to save time and to
ensure correct yardage and correct fit!

BACK

With MC, cast on 40 (46 - 50 - 54) sts. Work in k1, p1 rib for 2 rows. Work in St st and stripe pat until piece measures 10 (12 - 13 - 14)″ / 25 (30.5 - 33 - 35.5) cm from beg, end with a WS row. *Next row (RS):* Work 11 (13 - 15 - 16) sts and place on a holder for right shoulder, bind off next 18 (20 - 20 - 22) sts for neck, with MC, cont in St st on rem 11 (13 - 15 - 16) sts for 1″ / 2.5 cm for button placket. Bind off.

FRONT

Work same as back until piece measures 8 (10 - 11 - 12)″ / 20 (25.5 - 28 - 30.5) cm from beg, end with a WS row. **Shape neck:** *Next row (RS):* Work 15 (17 - 19 - 20) sts, place rem sts on a holder. Cont in stripe pat on left front sts only and bind off from neck edge 2 sts once, then dec 1 st every other row twice—11 (13 - 15 - 16) sts, and *at the same time,* when piece measures 9½ (11½ - 12½ - 13½)″ / 23.5 (29 - 31.5 - 34) cm from beg, end with a WS row and work shoulder as foll: *Next row (RS), buttonholes:*

STRIPE PATTERN

Work back and forth on circular needle as foll:

Note: Carry CC up sides for stripes.

Rows 1, 3, and 5 (RS): With MC, knit.

Rows 2 and 4: With MC, purl.

Row 6: With CC, purl. Slide sts back to other end of needle to work next row from WS.

Rows 7, 9, and 11 (WS): With MC, purl.

Rows 8 and 10: With MC, knit.

Row 12: With CC, knit. Slide sts back to other end needle to work next row from RS.

Rep rows 1–12 for stripe pat.

K 2 (3 - 3 - 3), k2tog, yo, k 3 (3 - 5 - 6), yo, k2tog, k to end. Cont in St st until same length as back. Bind off sts. With RS facing, rejoin yarn and bind off center 10 (12 - 12 - 14) sts for neck, work to end. Work neck shaping as for left side, omitting buttonholes. When same length as back, place sts on a holder for later finishing.

SHOULDER SEAMS

With *wrong sides facing* each other, and front of sweater facing you, place sts of back and front right shoulders on two parallel dpns. With a third dpn, k first stitch from front needle tog with first stitch from back needle, *k next stitch from front and back needles tog, sl first st over 2nd st to bind off; rep from * until all sts are bound off. Cut yarn and pull end through last loop.

Sew buttons to left shoulder.

SLEEVES

Mark for sleeves 5 (5½ - 6 - 6½)" / 12.5 (14 - 15.5 - 16.5) cm down from shoulder seam on front and back. With RS facing and MC, pick up and k 40 (44 - 48 - 52) sts between markers (working through both thicknesses on left side). Work in St st and stripe pat for 5 rows, then dec 1 st each end on next row, then every 6th row 3 (4 - 4 - 2) times more, every 4th row 3 (4 - 5 - 9) times, to 26 (26 - 28 - 28) sts. Work even until

sleeve measures 5½ (7 - 7½ - 8)" / 14 (17.5 - 19 - 20.5) cm, end with a RS row. With MC, work in k1, p1 rib for 2 rows, then bind off in rib loosely and evenly.

FINISHING

Sew side and sleeve seams. Sew button to neckband.

Neckband

With RS facing, circular needle and MC, beg at left front neck edge, pick up and k 58 (62 - 62 - 66) sts evenly around neck edge, including side of back button placket. Work in k1, p1 rib for 1 row. *Next row (RS), buttonhole:* Rib 2, yo, k2tog, rib rem sts. Work 1 more row of ribbing. Bind off in rib loosely and evenly.

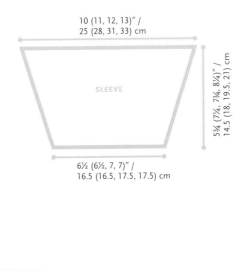

4½ (5, 5, 5½)" /
11.5 (12.5, 12.5, 14) cm

2 ¾ (3¼, 3¾, 4)" /
7 (8.5, 9.5, 10) cm

1" / 2.5 cm

2" / 5 cm

5 (5½, 6, 6½)" / 12.5 (14, 15.5, 16.5) cm

FRONT & BACK

8 (10, 11, 12)" / 20 (25.5, 28, 30.5) cm

5 (6½, 7, 7½)" / 12.5 (16.5, 17.5, 19) cm

10 (11½, 12½, 13½)" /
25.5 (29, 31.5, 34.5) cm

10 (11, 12, 13)" /
25 (28, 31, 33) cm

SLEEVE

5¾ (7¼, 7¾, 8¼)" / 14.5 (18, 19.5, 21) cm

6½ (6½, 7, 7)" /
16.5 (16.5, 17.5, 17.5) cm

merci mille fois

Any book is the result of the efforts of
a bevy of talented people, over many, many
months. Enormous, jubilant thanks to Nina
Fuller, who takes the adorable photos; to
Carla Scott, who exquisitely edits and writes
the patterns; to Judith Shangold, deft
pattern proofreader and editor; to Merle
Hagelin, who magically styles the miniature
models; and to Isabel Smiles, my overall
design guru.

ABOUT JIL ET AL.

After a multifaceted education in art at
Skidmore College, Colby College, and the
Graduate School of Design at Harvard
University, Jil Eaton's professional career as
painter, graphic designer, arts administrator,
and restaurateur has dressed her in many
hats, most lately as an internationally
acclaimed knitting designer. She designs,
publishes, and distributes internationally an
independent line of hand-knitting patterns
for children's wear under the MinnowKnits
label. A formidable knitter, Jil Eaton's
designs have a comfortable, but chic
silhouette, encompassing both the
traditional and the newest trends, adapting
everything into easy-to-knit projects with
great attention to detail, fresh styling, and
unusual colorways. Fascinated with color
and fashion, Jil's inspiration comes from
many diverse directions—from the pages of
French *Vogue* to paintings in the Met. Never

at a loss for ideas, Jil produces two
collections annually, designs for *Vogue
Knitting International* and other publications,
and is busy with her fifth book. Always
returning to her deep-seated love of knitting,
designing knitwear focuses all her talents.
Her spacious studios are clean and white,
full of sketches, drawings, photographs, and
mountains of delicious yarns. Jil juggles
work for the collections, travel, and life with
her financier husband David, her son
Alexander, and an enormous, sleek black
dog. And in spite of all the deadlines and
responsibilities inherent in such a busy life,
she still loves to knit!

Nina Van Brocklin Fuller is the one who
so wonderfully captures all these charming
models on film. A nationally acclaimed
location and studio photographer, Nina has
degrees from Silvermine College of Art and
George Washington University in
photography, painting, and printmaking.
After college, Nina worked the big time in
New York City, assisting the talented stock
photographer Nancy Brown and shooting,
shooting, shooting. . . . Always on her toes,

always with a camera in hand, Nina has a
gift for catching the right angle, finding the
most beautiful light, capturing the exact
moment when the tear falls or the smile
breaks. Location photography has emerged
as a creative focus for Nina, and her major
clients include L.L. Bean, Lands' End,
Atlantic Records, and last but not least,
MinnowKnits International. Her on-the-spot

location work with people is rarely matched, as her inimitable charm and energy transfix her beguiled subjects.

Nina lives in Maine with her two beautiful children, whom we often see through her camera lens. Growing up in the studio, constantly in front of one camera or another, both kids have a presence and inner light that is remarkably tangible. As does Nina.

After years of fashion and retail experience, Merle Hagelin decided to change her direction, and we're delighted she did. In beauty school for about 10 minutes, Merle drew instead on her many natural talents and instantly made quite a splash as a makeup artist in film and video. Her first makeup assignment was with Joe Brennan, the governor of the state of Maine, and was a springboard into a career filled with interesting personalities. She has used her magic wands on former President George Bush, baseball icon Ted Williams, "LA Law"'s Richard Dysart, wild and scary author Stephen King, and even the revered Martha Stewart! Her prestigious national and international clients include L.L. Bean,

Coca-Cola, NBC, CBS, AT&T, Atlantic Records, Bose Industries, Digital, and of course MinnowKnits International. Merle can finesse any situation, gets nervous models to breath and light up, and can make even the scruffiest curmudgeon beautiful. With her magic touch and smile, Merle is the best baby wrangler on the planet.

Isabel Smiles is my design sounding board as well as location stylist. She moved to Maine 10 years ago after a successful run as a stylist and antiques and design shop owner in New York and Connecticut, and she created the world-renowned Pomegranate Inn Bed and Breakfast, a stunning small

hotel in Portland, Maine. We have shot some of my earlier books in her landmark inn, and her wonderful rich rooms chock-full of art, antiques, hand-painted wall treatments, and other remarkable details, all put together with her unbelievably talented eye, have created backgrounds without compare. She continues to do select freelance styling for the Meredith Corporation and Hearst Publications, as well as private design commissions.

Carla Scott is my pattern writer, technical editor, and general knitting wizard. Practically born into the business, she is without peer in her fabulous knowledge of knitting and garment structure, and for many years has been able to translate my design concepts into written instructions and comprehensive charts. She lights up when presented with a new design challenge, figuring out details that practically make me faint. She is clear and calm amidst a mountain of math and engineering. Carla is senior editor at *Vogue Knitting*, and as always, she has made working on this project a delight.

Judith Shangold and Janice Bye are my pattern checkers and editors par excellence, and have the enormous task of reviewing all the patterns and charts at many different stages for accuracy and consistency. A designer herself, Judith publishes her own work under Designs by Judith and A Bear in Sheep's Clothing.

THE KNITTERS

Finding hand-knitters with an eye for perfection and professional craftsmanship is ever a challenge, and I have quite a merry band of intrepid knitters. We always have knitting emergencies, last-minute changes, and reknits. Knitting under fire can be exacting at best, nerve-racking at worst. We all work together, and the results of all the efforts are extraordinary.

Nita Young has fleet fingers and wonderful calm ways. Audrey Lewis and Lucinda Heller are my Fair Isle masters. Peggy Lewis knits with more alacrity than I have ever seen, perfectly to boot. Joan Cassidy knits elegantly, with the most beautifully finished garments around. Carol Gillis, my studio assistant, is also a fabulous knitter, problem solver, and designer. Nancy Cooper knit and felted the Felties hat and booties, and was my felting consultant; she designs and publishes under her Dancing Whiskers label. Starr Moore knits nimbly and has a wonderful eye for pattern nuances, giving us terrific feedback. Janice Bye, Charlotte Parry, and Shirley LaBranch round out the wildly talented group for this collection.

MODELS

This book has been fun and challenging, as the smaller the model, the more trying the photo shoot! This coterie of models was quite diverse, discovered among my friends and family and beyond. After creating a new collection, it is such a thrill to see the garments in real life on these darling kids.

Jump	Ellie Hamren Purgavie
Puff Baby	Arianna True
Genghis Baby	Fionn Desmond,
	McKenna Troast
Feltie Feet	Arianna True
Feltie Chapeau	Harriet Edwardsen,
	Isabella Perry,
	Lucia Helder

Snow Baby	Fionn Desmond, McKenna Troast	
Gelati	Lucia Helder	
Vestimenti	Axel Morgan	
Piccolo	Olivia Clifford, Isabella Perry	
English Trifle		
Dutch Treat	McKenna Troast	
"Tricks of the Trade"	Lily Hoffman	
Swing Set	Emma Stehli	
Seedling	Olivia Clifford	
Cable-Alls	Fionn Desmond	
Colori	John Alexandre	

Other enormous thanks go to my talented and charming literary agent, Sandy Taylor; to my extraordinary and esteemed editor, Anne Knudsen; and to my visionary art director, Kim Bartko. Thanks also to my mother, Nancy Whipple Lord, for teaching me to knit, and to my grandmother Flora Hall Whipple for teaching *her* to knit. Thanks to Carol Gillis, my studio assistant, for dauntlessly keeping everything on track and on schedule! Thanks a million to you all.

shopping notes

All the gorgeous yarns and products used
in this book are available from the following
stockists. You can contact them for shops in
your area. These companies provide some
of the most beautiful yarns on the market,
and you can depend on them for the highest
quality. Always knit with the very best yarns
and materials you can afford . . . remember,
you're knitting for posterity!

YARNS

BERROCO

14 Elmdale Road
P.O. Box 367
Uxbridge, MA 01569-0367

BROWN SHEEP

100662 County Road 16
Mitchell, NE 69357
www.brownsheep.com

MANOS DEL URUGUAY

Design Source, U.S. Distributor
38 Montvale, Suite 145
Stoneham, MA 02180

ROWAN YARNS

5 Northern Boulevard
Amherst, NH 03031
www.rowanyarns.co.uk

CRYSTAL PALACE

2320 Bissell Avenue
Richmond, CA 94804

UNIQUE KOLOURS

1428 Oak Lane
Downington, PA 19335

REYNOLDS

c/o JCA
35 Scales Lane
Townsend, MA 01469-1094

TRENDSETTER YARNS

16742 Stagg Street
Van Nuys, CA 91406

NEEDLES

ADDI TURBOS

Skacel Collection, Inc.
224 S.W. 12th Street
Renton, WA 98055

SWALLOW CASEIN

Design Source
38 Montvale Avenue, Suite 145
Stoneham, MA 02180

CRYSTAL PALACE

2320 Bissell Avenue
Richmond, CA 94804

BUTTONS

ZECCA

P.O. Box 1664
Lakeville, CT 06039
(hand-made Fimo buttons)
www.zecca.net

CENTRAL YARN

53 Oak Street
Portland, ME 04101

MINNOWKNITS PATTERNS

Distributed by DESIGN SOURCE

P.O. Box 770

Medford, MA 02155

(781) 438-9631; www.minnowknits.com

(available at fine yarn shops)

books of note

Books on knitting abound, but I have found a few to be particularly wonderful, full of insight, technical information, and design inspiration.

Editors of *Vogue Knitting, Vogue Knitting.* New York: Pantheon Books, 1989.
One of my favorites, this book is rich in history and is great for technique, with clear illustrations for just about everything. It is required for my knitting classes, and has good basic design information and some traditional patterns. If you just buy one book, buy this.

Hiatt, June Hemons. *The Principles of Knitting.* New York: Simon and Schuster, 1988.
This book is, unbelievably, out of print, but is wonderful if you can find it!

Goldberg, Rhoda Ochser. *The New Knitting Dictionary.* New York: Crown Publishers, 1984.

Newton, Deborah. *Designing Knitwear.* Newton, CT: Taunton Press, 1992.
A fabulous book on design, including history, technique, and new ways to see.

Norbury, James, and Margaret Aguter. *Oldhams Encyclopedia of Knitting.* London: Oldhams Books, Ltd., 1957.

Standfield, Lesley. *The New Knitting Stitch Library*. Radnor, PA: Chilton Book Company, 1992.
Comprehensive, with some new stitches for inspiration.

Stanley, Montse. *The Handknitter's Handbook*. London: David and Charles, 1986.
Great source for various cast-on techniques.

Square, Vicki. *The Knitter's Companion*. Loveland, CO: Interweave Press, 1996.
Tuck this into your knitting bag for a quick, convenient reference book.

Zimmerman, Elizabeth. *Knitter's Almanac*. New York: Charles Scribner's Sons, 1974. Reprint, New York: Dover Publications, 1981.

———. *Knitting Without Tears*. New York: Charles Scribner's Sons, 1971.

short stuff

ABBREVIATIONS

approx	approximately	psso	pass the slipped stitch over the last stitch worked
beg	beginning		
CC	contrasting color	rem	remaining
cont	continue(s) or continuing	rep	repeat(s)
cn	cable needle	rev St st	reverse stockinette stitch, k all WS rows, p all RS rows
dc	double crochet		
dec	decrease(s)	rib	rib(bing)
dpn	double pointed needle	rnd(s)	round(s) in circular knitting
est	established	RS	right side
foll	follows	sc	single crochet
inc(s)	increase(s)	sl	slip, slipped, or slipping; slip stitches from left-hand needle to right-hand needle
k	knit		
k2tog	knit two stitches together		
M	make	st(s)	stitch(es)
MC	main color	St st	stockinette stitch, k all RS rows, p all WS rows
p	purl		
p2tog	purl two stitches together	tog	together
pat(s)	patterns(s)	WS	wrong side
		yo	yarn over

needle conversions

Metric (mm)	US	Old UK	Metric (mm)	US	Old UK
2	0	14	5	8	6
2.25	1	13	5.5	9	5
2.5			6	10	4
2.75	2	12	6.5	10.5	3
3			7		2
3.25	3	10	7.5		1
3.5	4		8	11	0
3.75	5		9	13	00
4	6	8	10	15	000
4.5	7	7			

index

Abbreviations, 124
Addi Turbo circular needles, xi
Addi Turbos, 120
Aguter, Margaret, 122
Altering patterns, xiv

Baby Baby, 70–74
Baby Bunting, 12–16
Bamboo needles, xiii
Berroco, 118
Bind off, xxvii
Blanket, 8–11
Blocking, xxi–xxiii
Books on knitting, 122–23
Booties, 18–20
Brown Sheep, 118
Bunting with helmet,
        12–16
Buttons, 120

Cable-alls, 46–51
Cable needles, x
Calculator, x

Caps
    cardigan and overalls with cap, 46–51
    christening gown with caplet, 22–27
    jumpsuit with cap, 64–69
Cardigans, 36–39, 40–44, 80–83
    hooded, 70–74
    with overalls and cap, 46–51
Carriage blanket, 8–11
Cast on, xxv
Center-back-sleeve (CBS)
        measurements, xvii
Central Yarn, 120
Chenille yarn, vix
Chest measurements, xvii
Chibi needles, x
Christening gown with cap, 22–27
Circular needles, xi
Cold-weather wear, 60–83
    cardigan, 80–83
    hats, 60–62
    hooded cardigan, 70–74
    jumpsuit with cap, 64–69
    stocking hat, 76–79

Colori, 106–9

Colors, adding, xxi

Cotton yarn, vix

Crochet hooks, xi

Crystal Palace, 120

Design Source, 121

Designing Knitwear (Newton), 122

Double pointed needles, xiii

Dutch Treat, 52–57

English Trifle, 98–101

Eucalan, xxiii

Feltie Chapeau, 94–96

Feltie Feet, 18–20

Finishing, xxi

Flax Jax, 40–44

Garter stitch, xxvi

Gauge, viii, xx

Gauge swatches, xix–xx

Gelati, 90–93

Genghis Baby, 60–62

Girls

    jumper or sundress, 102–5

    swing top and diaper cover, 30–34

Goldberg, Rhoda Ochser, 122

The Handknitter's Handbook (Stanley), 123

Hats, 60–62

    madeleine, 94–96

    measurements, xvii

Hiatt, June Hemons, 122

Hooded cardigan, 70–74

Increase, xxvii

Jump, 64–69

Jumper, 102–5

Jumpsuit with cap, 64–69

Kimono, 2–6

Knit 2 together (k2tog), xxvii, 124

Knit stitch, xxv–xxvi

Knitter's Almanac (Zimmerman), 123

The Knitter's Companion (Square), 123

Knitting bag or basket, xi

Knitting lights, xiv

Knitting notebook, xiii

Knitting supplies, x–xiv

Knitting Without Tears, 123

Koko Kimono, 2–6

Laundering, xxiii

Layette, 1–27

    bunting with helmet, 12–16

    carriage blanket, 8–11

    christening gown with cap, 22–27

    felted booties, 18–20

    kimono, 2–6

Lights, knitting, xiv

Madeleine hat, 94–96

Manos Del Uruguay, 120

Measurements, xiv–xv, xvii

Measuring tape, x

Mini Pini, 102–5

Minnowknits patterns, 121

Needle cases, xiii

Needle/gauge ruler, xi

Needles, x, xi

    conversions, 125

    sources, 120

The New Knitting Dictionary

    (Goldberg), 122

The New Knitting Stitch Library

    (Standfield), 123

New yarn, adding, xxi

Newton, Deborah, 122

Norbury, James, 122

Notebook, knitting, xiii

Oldhams Encyclopedia of Knitting

    (Norbury and Aguter), 122

Overalls, 46–51

Piccolo, 80–83

Play clothes, 29–57

    cardigan, 36–39, 40–44

    cardigan, overalls and cap, 46–51

    pullover and trousers, 52–57

    swing top and diaper cover, 30–34

Point protectors, x

The Principles of Knitting (Hiatt), 122

Puff Baby, 8–11

Pullovers, 90–93, 98–101, 106–9
    and trousers, 52–57
Purl stitch, xxvi

Quickknits
    blanket, 8–11
    bunting with helmet, 12–16
    cardigan, 36–39, 40–44, 80–83
    cardigan, overalls and cap, 46–51
    felted booties, 18–20
    hats, 60–62
    hooded cardigan, 70–74
    jumper or sundress, 102–5
    jumpsuit with cap, 64–69
    kimono, 2–6
    madeleine hat, 94–96
    pullover, 106–9
    stocking hat, 76–79
    swing top and diaper cover, 30–34
    vest, 86–89

Reynolds, 120
Row counter, x
Row counting, xxi
Rowan Yarns, 120

Safety pins, x
Scissors, x
Seedling, 36–39
Selvage stitches, xv
Shoulder to waist measurements, xvii
Sizes, xv
Sleeves, xiv, xxi
Slip knot, xxiv
Snow Baby, 76–79
Square, Vicki, 123
Standfield, Lesley, 123
Stanley, Montse, 123
Stitch holders, x
Stitch markers, x
Stitches, xxiv–xxvii
Stockinette stitch, xxvi
Stocking hat, 76–79
Sundress, 102–5
Swallow Casein, 120
Swallow Casein needles, xi, xiii
Swing Set, 30–34
Swing top and diaper cover, 30–34

T-pins, x
Trendsetter Yarns, 120

Unique Kolours, 120

Unisex

blanket, 8–11

bunting with helmet, 12–16

cardigan, 36–39, 40–44, 80–83

cardigan, overalls and cap, 46–51

christening gown with cap, 22–27

felted booties, 18–20

hats, 60–62

hooded cardigan, 70–74

jumpsuit with cap, 64–69

kimono, 2–6

madeleine hat, 94–96

pullover, 90–93, 98–101, 106–9

pullover and trousers, 52–57

stocking hat, 76–79

vest, 86–89

Vest, 86–89

Vestimenti, 86–89

Vogue Knitting, 122

Waist measurements, xvii

Washing, xxiii

Welcome, Baby, 22–27

Wool yarn, vix

Yardage, yarn, vii

Yarn blends, vix

Yarn winder, xiii–xiv

Yarns, vix

    sources, 118–20

Zecca, 120

Zimmerman, Elizabeth, 122